MY LIFE
the screenplay

Written and Directed by
Bruce Joel Rubin

HARVEST MOON PUBLISHING

SANTA MONICA

MY LIFE: THE SCREENPLAY

The Script Publishing Project
Volume I Issue 39
July 2000

All rights reserved.
Copyright © 2000 by Harvest Moon Publishing®

No part of this publication may reproduced, transmitted, stored, or utilized in any form or
by any means electronic or mechanical, including photocopying, recording, or by any
information storage and retrieval system without written permission from the publisher,
except in the case of brief quotations embodied in critical articles and reviews.

Inquiries concerning amateur or professional acting
rights of this work should be directed to the producing studio.

The writing credit presented on this publication is identical to the writing credit of the final
production as determined by the Writers Guild of America. The writing credit may not
include writers who have contributed, in part or in entirety, to the final production. The
written script presented in this publication may not be identical to the final production.

ISBN 1-929750-93-5
ISSN: 1524-2056

Published in the United States by Harvest Moon Publishing®
in association with The Writers Guild Foundation™

Harvest Moon Publishing®	**The Writers Guild Foundation™**
P.O. Box 3332	7000 W. 3rd Street
Santa Monica, CA 90408	Los Angeles, CA 90048
1-877-7-HARVEST	
1-877-742-7837	

www.harvestmoon.com
online@harvestmoon.com

ABOUT THE SCRIPT PUBLISHING PROJECT

Why we do what we do

Harvest Moon Publishing, in association with the Writers Guild Foundation, established the Script Publishing Project in 1998 in an effort to give the public greater access to the works of film and television writers. The Project enjoys the support of writers and studios and, through Harvest Moon, maintains the largest catalog of script titles of any publisher. In addition, Project sales raise funds for the Foundation, a non-profit corporation dedicated to preserving and promoting the craft of writing.

How we do what we do

Unlike other publications, Harvest Moon scripts are published in their true format: pages are 8½ by 11 inches with the words printed on only one side of the page. These works are published just as the writers wrote them; they are not summarized or revised in any way. The principle behind the true format approach is that, like the layout of a poem, the way in which the words are set down on the page can dramatically affect the way a script is read.

To find out more

Harvest Moon Publishing continues to add new film screenplays and television scripts to its catalog. To learn more about The Script Publishing Project or to receive an up-to-date list of available titles, contact:

Harvest Moon Publishing
P.O. Box 3332
Santa Monica, CA 90408

1-877-7-HARVEST
1-877-742-7837

www.harvestmoon.com
online@harvestmoon.com

ABOUT THE WRITERS GUILD FOUNDATION

The Writers Guild Foundation was established in 1966 as a non-profit charitable corporation by a group of television and motion picture writers, members of the Writers Guild of America, west. The founding president was James. R. Webb.

THE FOUNDATION'S MISSION IS:

- to promote and encourage excellence in writing;
- to educate the public concerning the role of the writer in film and television;
- to preserve the work of film and television writers and thereby to create a significant historical resource for future generations;
- to encourage the further education of writers; and
- to promote communication between writers.

THE FOUNDATION'S CURRENT MAJOR PROGRAMS ARE:

- The James R. Webb Memorial Library, housing over 4,000 award nominated scripts and a reference collection of books, tapes and photographs related to writers and writing, and to the history of writers in Hollywood;

- *The Writer Speaks*, a series of oral history interviews on video with the great writers of film and television;

- *Words*, a short film highlighting and celebrating the writer's contribution to some of the great moments in motion pictures;

- Seminars and tributes, including its annual Career Achievement Award;

- An academic liaison program with schools and colleges;

- Conferences and international exchanges, including Words Into Pictures, a biennial forum for film and television writers.

TO FIND OUT MORE:

The Foundation's activities are funded by voluntary contributions from writers and industry friends. To learn more, or to find out how you can contribute, contact:

THE WRITERS GUILD FOUNDATION
(323) 782-4692

MY LIFE

An Original Screenplay

By

Bruce Joel Rubin

March 3, 1993

1   EXT. SUBURBAN NEIGHBORHOOD - EVENING   1

It is dusk. BOBBIE, a young boy about six years old, scampers through a backyard, across an alley, and into an open field in his pajamas and slippers. He keeps glancing up at the sky, searching for something. Suddenly, squinting, he sees it, a faint star making its first appearance in the slate blue darkness of evening. There is a thrill on BOBBIE'S face. Slowly he intones what is for him a prayer.

      BOBBIE
  Star light, star bright, first star
  I see tonight, I wish I may, I wish
  I might, have the wish I wish
  tonight.
    (his eyes closing)
  Dear God, please, please, I want
  there to be a circus in my backyard
  tomorrow when I get home from
  school. Not a fake circus. A real
  circus, with clowns, and acrobats,
  and everything. Please. I believe
  in you. I believe in wishes.
    (suddenly the prayer
     turns into a sales
     pitch)
  If you do this I'll tell everybody.
  It'll be good for you. It'll be on
  television and in the newspapers.
  You'll get more money at church.
  Please God, please. Make this come
  true.

A shrill voice cuts through the cool night air.

      ROSE (O.S.)
  Bobbie! You get in here this
  minute. You hear me? I'm countin'
  to five. I mean it.

There is a panicked look on BOBBIE'S face. He turns and rushes through the field.

      ROSE (O.S.)
    (continuing)
  One! Two!

2   EXT. TRACT HOUSE - EVENING   2

BOBBIE dashes toward a small two story house. A 1960 Chevrolet pickup truck is parked in the driveway. His MOTHER, a Ukrainian peasant woman, is standing in the doorway, yelling.

              (CONTINUED)

2   CONTINUED: 2

                         ROSE
                     (continuing)
            Three! You're gonna get it. Four!

Hearing something, she glances toward the back of the house
and sees BOBBIE rushing into the side door.

3   INT. TRACT HOUSE - EVENING   3

BOBBIE shoots into the kitchen and sees his mother coming
toward him down the hall. He escapes, detouring through the
dining and living rooms. His father, BILL, a balding man in
his early thirties, is sprawled out in the living room
chair. He looks up.

                         BILL
            What'dja do now?

BOBBIE doesn't answer. Grabbing hold of the globe on the
tip of the banister, he swings himself onto the stairs and
races up to his bedroom.

4   INT. BOBBIE'S BEDROOM - EVENING   4

BOBBIE jumps into his bed, rapidly pulling the covers up
over his head. We hear ROSE yelling at BILL in the living
room.

                         ROSE (O.S.)
            Whataya just lie there for? He's
            your kid too you know.

We hear her marching angrily up the stairs. BOBBIE'S little
brother PAUL sits up unexpectedly.

                         PAUL
            Oh oh. Mommy's gonna spank you.

ROSE comes huffing and puffing into the room. She walks
over to the bed and takes a series of indiscriminate swipes
at BOBBIE'S rump buried somewhere under the blanket.

                         BOBBIE
            Didn't hurt.

                         PAUL
                     (excited)
            Do it again Mom.

                         ROSE
                     (to PAUL)
            You want a smack in the head?

PAUL shakes his head "no".

                                                     (CONTINUED)

4   CONTINUED: 4

                            ROSE
                       (continuing)
                  Go to sleep, both of you. And no
                  more monkey business, y'hear?

She slams the door. After a moment we hear a strange ping
off the brick wall and then a voice calling out. It is
CAROL SANDMAN, the girl next door.

                            CAROL
                  Hey, Bobbie, open up.

BOBBIE opens the window. We see CAROL, age 8, in her
bedroom across the way. She is holding a new B.B. gun in
her hand.

                            BOBBIE
                  Hey, Carol. Where'd you get that?

                            CAROL
                  My Uncle Herbert. He bought it for
                  my brother. Neat huh?

                            BOBBIE
                  Really neat! Now you can shoot
                  your piano teacher.
                       (Carol smiles)
                  Just kidding.

                            VOICE
                       (from inside CAROL'S
                        house)
                  Do I hear talking up there?

                            CAROL
                  Yikes. Gotta go.

CAROL dives under her covers. BOBBIE smiles and is about to
lie back down when he notices his brother sitting up in bed.
BOBBIE turns to him.

                            BOBBIE
                  Hey, you wanna know a secret?
                  You're not gonna believe what's
                  gonna happen tomorrow, right in our
                  own backyard.

                            PAUL
                  What? Tell me.

                            BOBBIE
                  I can't.

                                                      (CONTINUED)

4   CONTINUED: 2   4

                    PAUL
          Please? Pretty please.

                    BOBBIE
               (shaking his head "no")
          You just wait...tomorrow
          afternoon...you'll see. Something
          great.

                    PAUL
          I don't believe you.

                    BOBBIE
          Cross my heart and hope to die.
          Stick a needle in my eye.

There is an expectant look on PAUL'S face. He smiles
excitedly and hops under the sheets.

5   INT. FIRST GRADE CLASSROOM - DAY   5

THE CAMERA PANS A ROOM full of young, eager faces in a first
grade classroom. A picture of President Kennedy hangs on the
rear wall. BOBBIE is standing in front of the class writing
his address and phone number on the blackboard. A SUBSTITUTE
TEACHER stands nearby. Her name, MISS MORGENSTERN, is also
written on the board.

                    MISS MORGENSTERN
          Okay children, tear a page neatly
          from your notebook and then copy the
          address down just as it's written.

Several of the children respond diligently, writing the
address for Bobbie Ivanovich in large block letters.

                    MISS MORGENSTERN
               (continuing)
          Isn't this exciting? How many
          children have relatives in the
          circus? I'll bet your regular
          teacher wishes she was here today.

                    BOBBIE
          There'll be clowns, and a trapeze,
          horses and everything.

                    MISS MORGENSTERN
          All in your back yard. Isn't that
          thrilling?

                                                      (CONTINUED)

5   CONTINUED:

A few of the boys look at each other and roll their eyes in disbelief.

> BOBBIE
> And everyone from school gets in free.

> MISS MORGENSTERN
> Be sure to put down the time. Do you know how to write 3:30? It's very easy.

She steps to the board and writes it down.

CUT TO THE SOUND OF THE SCHOOL BELL RINGING

6   OMIT

7   OMIT

8   EXT. SCHOOL - DAY

The school door flies open and BOBBIE is the first one out. He heads rapidly across the front lawn as someone yells at him to "wait up". He doesn't listen.

9   EXT. IVANOVICH 50'S NEIGHBORHOOD - DAY

THE CAMERA TRACKS CLOSE TO THE GROUND following BOBBIE'S footsteps as he runs down the sidewalk, consciously avoiding the cracks. The houses rush by him, small tract homes in a blue collar neighborhood. Several boys drive by on their bicycles, playing cards clicking noisily in the spokes of their wheels.

BOBBIE'S house approaches. THE CAMERA SPEEDS TOWARD IT.

CLOSE UP ON BOBBIE'S FACE. His lips are moving in silent prayer.

PAUL is standing on the front porch railing, a towel tied around his neck like a Superman cape. He sees his brother and jumps over the bushes onto the grass. BOBBIE speeds past him, heading toward the backyard.

> PAUL
> Where're you going? Is this the surprise?

10 EXT. IVANOVICH 50'S BACKYARD - DAY

FROM THE CAMERA'S P.O.V. we rush past the back gate and enter a world of dazzling color. For an instant we sense that something magical has occurred but then we realize that the billowing fabrics are only the family wash hanging on the line. There is no circus.

BOBBIE stops short, out of breath. He stares into the yard in a state of confusion and betrayal. Suddenly a hand grabs him by the shoulder. He spins around. His mother is towering over him. She is not happy. Behind her, in the entrance to the yard, MISS MORGENSTERN, a group of mothers and their children are standing curiously.

> ROSE
> What is this circus? Where is this circus?

BOBBIE just stands there, amazed and humiliated.

> BOBBIE
> I don't know. It was supposed to be here. It was supposed to come.

Tears form in his eyes as he pulls away and runs toward the house. His classmates eye him oddly as he rushes past them and hurries inside. PAUL watches his brother, sadly.

11 INT. BOBBIE'S BEDROOM - DAY

BOBBIE hurries into his room and runs into a tiny storage closet cut into the attic wall. He sits there beside old wrapping paper and a stash of his private toys. A tiny crack of light shows the tears running down his cheeks. After a moment he leans over and pulls the door shut. It closes with a powerful and unexpected finality. The screen goes black.

OPENING CREDITS

12 INT. JONES BEDROOM - DAY

A VIDEO IMAGE of a large and stylish bedroom bleeds into focus. A comfortable winged-back chair dominates the view.

We can hear sounds of fidgeting in the background and then a MAN'S BODY appears filling the screen. He sits down and we are about to glimpse his face when the camera slips, tilts forward, and focuses on his feet.

The feet leave the frame and the image tilts back up to the chair. The man returns and sits down. Now we see him clearly.

(CONTINUED)

12   CONTINUED: 12

He is a good looking man, probably in his mid-30's, but he
seems tired beyond his years. He does not look particularly
healthy or comfortable. He glances off screen at a T.V.
monitor. We see him looking at himself. Somewhat self
consciously, he fixes his hair and adjusts his jacket and tie.
He does not like the way he looks.

After a moment of unsatisfactory primping the man turns back
to the camera. He seems to want to say something but does
not know how to start. His eyes dart uncomfortably around
the room. After several seconds of abject failure, he
flashes the remote control at the camera and the image goes
dead.

ANOTHER SETUP. A new image appears. The man is in a new
jacket, this time without his tie. He still seems
uncomfortable. Curiously, he aims the remote control at the
camera and pushes the zoom lens control. Instantly the
image begins zooming toward him. Unfortunately, it does not
stop at his face but ends up focused on the curtains behind
him. Click to blackness.

ANOTHER SETUP. The man is now wearing a sport jacket and
plaid shirt, less formal than before. It takes him a moment
to look almost comfortable. Finally, with great hesitation,
he begins.

                              MAN
                           (serious)
                    Hello, my name is Robert Jones.

That's as far as he gets. He is not happy. With a click of
the remote he turns off the camera. The screen goes black.

12A   A NEW ANGLE   12A

A moment later the camera clicks back on again. BOB has
rearranged his position in the chair as if trying to look
more casual, comfortable. He starts over.

                              MAN
                    Hi, my name is Jones. Bobbie Jones.
                    Formerly Ivanovich.
                         (he pauses)
                    Formerly Ivanovich-smirnov-
                    stolychinaya-owski... Just kidding.

He shakes his head again. Still not right. The screen goes
blank.

12B   A NEW ANGLE   12B

The man's image reappears. The chair has been repositioned in another corner of the room.

                    MAN
              (earnestly)
       Hi. My name is Bob Jones.
              (he hesitates, unsure)
       Look, I'll be honest with you. I
       haven't the slightest idea what I'm
       trying to do here.
              (stopping abruptly)
       Damn!... I don't know how to start
       this...
              (after a long
               hesitation)
       I'm sorry...this is very difficult
       for me.

He pauses awkwardly. Suddenly the phone rings. A look of annoyance flashes across his face as he gets up from the chair. It is a shock to see that he is not wearing pants, just a jacket, shirt, and underwear.

                    BOB (V.O.)
       Hello... No. This is Bob... No,
       you didn't wake me... Whataya mean
       she cancelled the tour? We've been
       promoting this thing for three
       months. Son-of-a-bitch. Look, hold
       on a second, okay?

CUT BACK TO THE VIDEO IMAGE as BOB crosses in front of the screen in a rapid blur. We hear the sound of a button being pushed and the screen goes blank.

12C   A NEW ANGLE   12C

CUT TO BOB, back in the chair. We can tell from the mid-afternoon sunlight that time has passed. He is now in khakis and a button down shirt. It takes him several seconds to begin talking.

                    BOB
       Hi, my name is Robert Alan Jones.
       Most people call me Bob.
              (he rolls his eyes
               disapprovingly)
       ...I was born on April 10, 1956.
       In Detroit, Michigan. I am 36
       years old.
                  (MORE)

(CONTINUED)

12C CONTINUED:

>   BOB (cont'd)
>   (grimacing)
>   I'd like to tell you a little bit
>   about myself.
>   (thinking)
>   Not that I know what to say...
>   (pause)
>   I went to James Vernor Elementary
>   School, named after the ginger ale.
>   We used to get free Vernor's ginger
>   ale every Christmas. In those days
>   they only sold Vernor's in Detroit.
>   Now you can get it here in L.A. I
>   bought some at Hughes Market just
>   last month. Still tastes great.
>   (this is not going
>   well)
>   Am I puttin' you to sleep yet?
>   (shaking his head)
>   So...I graduated Henry Ford High
>   School in 1974. Every Christmas
>   they'd give us a free Ford...just
>   kidding. I got an MBA at the
>   University of Michigan in ...'80.
>   (MORE)

(CONTINUED)

12C CONTINUED: 12C

>   BOB (cont'd)
>   I moved to Los Angeles in 1981 and
>   founded R. A. Jones Public
>   Relations Inc., in '82.

We can tell he is not happy with this.

>   BOB
>   (continuing)
>   Goddamn! What is this? A fucking
>   resume? Shit!

He grabs a book and throws it at the camera. The image spins as the camera collapses to the floor with a huge thud. The screen goes blank.

13   OMIT   13

14   EXT. LOS ANGELES HOME - LATE AFTERNOON   14

The video image of a stylish Cheviot Hills home appears on screen as seen from across the street.

>   BOB (V.O.)
>   Okay, it's working. I think it's
>   working.
>   (he begins walking)
>   This is my house. Our house. I'm
>   walking toward it. 19386 Tracey
>   Ave. Beautiful street. Great park
>   around the corner. You're gonna
>   love it here.

15   EXT. JONES BEDROOM VERANDA - SUNSET   15

We see a view of the Jones' back yard from the upstairs porch. BOB is pacing back and forth through the frame. An orange glow fills the air. The sun is setting. After a moment, he stops. There is a serious and determined expression on his face. He stares at the camera and starts to talk.

>   BOB
>   Look, I'd like to do this in some
>   kind of polished way, but it's just
>   not coming out like that. So
>   you're just going to have to settle
>   for it like this.
>   (MORE)

                                                              (CONTINUED)

15 CONTINUED: 15

>   BOB (cont'd)
>   (pause)
>   I've always been better expressing
>   myself on paper, and maybe I should
>   have written this, but I wanted you
>   to see me...to know me...in the
>   flesh.
>   (pause)
>   I'm making this videotape... as a
>   way...of introducing myself.
>   (beat)
>   I really wish...we could have met.
>   (he pauses again,
>   growing very quiet)
>   My name is Bob Jones. I'm
>   your...father.

The word "father" catches in his throat. He swallows back a surge of emotion that catches him by surprise. Speechless, he shakes his head, not sure what to say.

>   BOB
>   (continuing)
>   Now what...?
>   (awkward pause)
>   It's funny. I'm a public relations
>   man. I've promoted Hollywood
>   stars, athletes, perfumes, you name
>   it...but I'll be damned if I know
>   how to promote myself.

Suddenly GAIL, BOB'S wife, calls upstairs.

>   GAIL (V.O.)
>   Honey, I'm home. Are you upstairs?

>   BOB
>   (calling back)
>   I'm right here.

>   GAIL (V.O.)
>   Are you okay?

>   BOB
>   I'm alright.

>   GAIL (V.O.)
>   What are you doing?.

>   BOB
>   Nothing.

The camera clicks off and the picture goes dead.

| 16 | INT. JONES HOUSE - EVENING | 16 |

BOB walks down the stairs through a lovely living and dining room, and into a beautifully appointed kitchen.

| 17 | INT. JONES KITCHEN - EVENING | 17 |

GAIL, 34, an attractive woman in a dark business suit, is taking some frozen dinners out of the refrigerator.

                    GAIL
                (turning to kiss him)
      Hi honey. How's it going?

BOB shrugs. We watch as he opens a pair of sliding doors revealing a family room beyond. Then, gently, he lowers himself into a chair at the kitchen table.

                    GAIL
                (continuing)
      You get much rest?

                    BOB
      A little.

                    GAIL
      Feeling any better? Medication
      helping?

BOB rotates his hand in a so-so gesture. GAIL shows concern. She pulls a head of lettuce from the vegetable crisper and begins chopping it into a salad.

                    GAIL
                (continuing)
      The Fenton deal went through.
      Everything's cleared. There's just
      a few glitches in the TV stuff, but
      nobody's worrying. By the way, Ron
      Heyzer says hello. They're
      promoting him. Managing Editor.
      That'll be good for us.

                    BOB
      That's great.

                    GAIL
      You want me to stop talking?

He shakes his head no.

                    BOB
      How was his toupee today?

                                  (CONTINUED)

17 CONTINUED: 17

                    GAIL
               (smiling)
          A little left of center. I mean
          really, what do you say to a guy
          when his head turns one way and his
          hair goes another?
               (turning suddenly)
          Oh...

She reaches into her purse and pulls out a bottle of
medicine.

                    GAIL
          Here's the new prescription from Dr.
          Califano. But be forewarned.
               (she reads from the
                medical packaging)
          "It may cause low blood pressure,
          rapid heart beat, swelling,
          itching, dry skin, rash, diarrhea,
          nausea, and dry mouth."

                    BOB
          Say anything about impotency?

                    GAIL
          Nope.

                    BOB
          Lemme have it.

Gail laughs and hands him the container. He pops a pill.

                    GAIL
          No water?

                    BOB
          Real men don't need water.

Suddenly he begins to cough and choke. Gail looks
concerned. Bob starts to laugh.

                    BOB
          Just kidding.

Gail shakes her head and goes back to making salad.

                    GAIL
          David asked if there was any chance
          you'd drop by his office tomorrow.
          He offered to come by the house but
          said that if you were going to be in
          the area it would make it easier for
          him.

                                                      (CONTINUED)

17 CONTINUED: 2

                    BOB
          Yeah, that's just what we want to
          do, make it easier for Dave.

                    GAIL
          There are tons of papers that need
          to be signed, the will, the
          mortgage transfer.

                    BOB
          He's really panicking, huh?

                    GAIL
          Bob...it has to get done.

                    BOB
          I'll let you know, okay?

GAIL nods and reaches down to pull off her shoes.

                    GAIL
          My feet have been swelling. I
          didn't think that happened till your
          seventh or eight month.

He watches her trying to manage five things at once.

                    BOB
          We could still go out to dinner.

                    GAIL
          I thought you wanted home cooking.

She tosses the frozen food containers into the microwave.

                    BOB
          That's home cooking...?

                    GAIL
              (stopping, angry)
          Listen you, you're the one who
          insisted that one of us keep going
          into the office. I'd rather stay
          home and cook for you any day and
          you know it. So don't complain
          about my cooking, okay? This was
          your idea.

                    BOB
          Whew?
              (they look at each
               other and smile)
          Look, come here, okay?
              (he taps his lap)
          Why don't you sit down?

(CONTINUED)

17 CONTINUED: 3   17

                         GAIL
            In just a sec. Let me get out of
            this.
                    (she unzips her skirt
                     and lets out a huge
                     sigh)
            Ohhh, that feels good.
                    (the skirt drops to her
                     feet and she kicks it
                     away)
            Well, so much for that suit.
                    (she feels her tummy
                     bulging beneath her
                     pantyhose)
            I gotta go shopping. It's getting
            embarrassing. I'm at that point
            where people are afraid to ask, "Is
            she getting fat, or...what?" I
            don't think anyone even thinks of me
            having children. After all these
            years, you know. I'm just one of
            the boys.

                         BOB
            Not to me.

                         GAIL
                    (on reflection)
            I hope not.

    GAIL smiles and sits on her husband's lap. Gently, with
    poignant and deeply felt tenderness, she strokes his head.

18 INT. JONES BEDROOM - NIGHT   18

    BOB and GAIL are in bed, awake, staring at the ceiling.
    After a few moments, BOB begins to speak.

                         BOB
            Eleanor called today...asked if I'd
            be treasurer again next year.

                         GAIL
            What did you say?

                         BOB
            What could I say? "I'm going
            fishing for the next hundred and
            fifty years"?

                                                              (CONTINUED)

18   CONTINUED: 18

                    GAIL
          Very funny. You know, at some point
          we're going to have to...tell
          people...

                    BOB
          Yeah, right. Be sure and tell me
          when that is.

                    GAIL
               (silence)
          Amazing isn't it? There's just no
          appropriate etiquette for this.
          What did you tell Eleanor?

                    BOB
          I just said there was too much
          happening with the business and that
          I couldn't plan.

                    GAIL
          That sounds good.
               (she squeezes his hand)

                    BOB
          You know, there must be some clever
          way to tell people you're dying.

                    GAIL
          You'd think Hallmark would've come
          up with something by now.

                    BOB
          Yeah, like, "Due to an unexpected
          terminal illness, Bob Jones regrets
          to inform you..."
               (Gail smiles)
          Or maybe I should change the
          answering machine. "Hi, this is Bob
          Jones speaking. I'm dead right now,
          but if you'll leave your name,
          number, and the time that you
          called..."

BOB doesn't finish. With shocking suddenness, BOB'S entire
body recoils and he begins to gasp. He can barely breathe.
His hand lurches out and grabs, onto the sheets with such
force that he rips them from the bed. GAIL jumps up and
tries to rub his back. BOB blocks her hand. He doesn't
want anyone touching him. A heavy sweat breaks out on his
forehead.

                                              (CONTINUED)

18 CONTINUED: 2   18

                              BOB
                    I hate this! I hate it!

GAIL grabs BOB'S medication from his nightstand and helps
shove a pill into his mouth. He swallows it instantly.

                                                  (CONTINUED)

18 CONTINUED: 2   18

We can tell from the look in her eyes that she shares his
pain. Slowly, he begins to relax.

                    BOB
               (continuing)
          This is ridiculous. I don't have
          time for this.

GAIL smiles as she helps BOB lower himself back down to his
pillow. Gently, she lies down beside him and strokes his
head. It's obvious that she loves this man.

19 INT. JONES BATHROOM SHOWER - NIGHT   19

A RUSH OF WATER surges toward the screen, steaming up the
shower door. A hand appears, its palm pressed against the
glass. It slides slowly down it, leaving a track through
the steam. Through it we see GAIL crouched at the bottom of
the stall. She is crying silently, careful not to utter a
sound. The flow of her tears mixes with the spray.

20 INT. JONES BEDROOM - DAY   20

A blank screen melts into BOB'S image. He is sitting once
again in the winged-back chair. His face nearly fills the
frame. Suddenly he blurts out.

                    BOB
          Look, I'm just going to do this.
          Okay? I'm sorry if it's not funny,
          or if it doesn't all make sense, but
          I don't have a lot of time to do it
          right.

He pauses for a moment and then charges ahead.

                    BOB
          The fact is, I'm supposed to be
          dying. I've a disease called
          cancer. There are many kinds of
          cancer. Mine started in my kidneys
          and has spread to my lungs. The
          doctor's trying some experimental
          therapies but he does not expect me
          to live very long. I plan to prove
          him wrong.
               (reflective pause)
          The tricky part, though, is not
          that they say I'm dying. It's that
          you are about to be born.
                    (MORE)

                                                      (CONTINUED)

CONTINUED:

> BOB (cont'd)
> The fact is we all die, and anything could happen to anybody. I could be hit by a truck tomorrow, right? A palm tree could crash through the bedroom roof and kill me in my sleep. But if something did happen, it'd be very hard 'cause there are a lot of things I want to tell you.
> (he pauses)
> The truth is, you can't trust very much in this screwed up world, so I figured even through I may not get a chance to meet you, you might want to know a little about me, about who your father...is. So I'm making this tape, for better or for worse, to leave some of me behind.
> (he pauses)
> Well...this is me.

CUT TO A BABY BOOK, obviously many years old. The lettering on the faded blue cover is flaking off. The book opens and the camera scans the pages and photos inside. BOB'S finger points to one of the pictures.

> BOB (V.O.)
> There I am. I weighed 8 lbs., 9oz. when I entered this world and was twenty-one inches long. Eyes brown, hair...none.
> (he turns the page and
> sees a tiny footprint)
> Look at that foot. Can you believe it?

He takes off his sock and puts his naked foot next to his own baby imprint. It is shocking to see the difference. He turns the camera on himself.

> BOB
> (continuing)
> Amazing. How's that even possible?
> (he turns the camera
> back to more photos)
> There I am with my mother, Rose. She said twelve tornados hit Detroit the day I was born. Four people were killed. It was symbolic. To her I was a born disaster. Still am...but that's for later. First things first.

(CONTINUED)

20 CONTINUED: 2   20

WE SEE A PHOTO of BILL, BOB'S father.

                    BOB
              (continuing)
          That's my dad, Bill. Pay attention.
          It's one of the few photos of him
          awake.
                    (we see another photo
                     of BILL, asleep on the
                     couch)
          You see? To get him off the couch,
          you had to tell him the sale light
          was flashing at K-Mart.

TURN TO A PHOTO OF BILL AND ROSE in front of a junkyard
fence. A hand painted sign says "Ivanovich Scrap Metal".

                    BOB
              (continuing)
          That's where my dad worked. Day
          and night. Ivanovich Scrap Metal.
          We hardly saw him.

21 EXT. NEIGHBORHOOD PARK - DAY   21

OLD HOME MOVIES flicker on the screen: aunts, uncles, and
cousins are at a picnic. They wave self-consciously to the
camera.

                    BOB (V.O.)
          These neolithic life forms are your
          relatives...grazing and foraging in
          Detroit. Most of them still live
          there so chances are you won't see
          them very often. Consider that a
          blessing. I wanted to show them to
          you because I think it's important
          to realize that who you are isn't
          necessarily all your fault. You can
          blame most of it on the gene pool.
          Apparently ours was polluted.

BOBBIE and PAUL are swinging side by side on a large swing
in a 1960's playground. Cousins are everywhere. They seem
very happy.

                    BOB
          That's me and your uncle, my
          brother Paul and some of our
          cousins...Nadia, Tania. We're
          busy learning important skills for
          our adult life...like swinging.

                                                      (CONTINUED)

21 CONTINUED: 21

Some overweight relatives are playing basketball badly and mugging for the camera.

> BOB
> These are assorted uncles and in-laws. As you can tell from these movies, the odds of a Reebok contract in your future are pretty slim.

22 EXT. EDGEWATER PARK - ROLLER COASTER 50'S - DAY 22

A splice and we cut to an amusement park in the early 1960's. A group of kids is piling out of a Pontiac station wagon. We recognize BOBBIE, about age 6. His UNCLE LOUIS, a large jolly man, is with them.

> BOB
> That's us with Uncle Louis and Aunt Tekla at Edgewater Park. They used to pack all of us into the back of their station wagon and take us on outings.

We see BOBBIE standing beside a huge roller coaster. He is crying. AUNT TEKLA is laughing and trying to comfort him at the same time. Other cousins are seen with cotton candy and all day suckers. They are making fun of him.

> BOB
> That's me and Tekla in front of the Screamer. My first and last roller coaster ride. All I remember was my Uncle Louis saying, "this is going to be fun". I thought I was going to die. It was at that moment I learned the meaning of the word "fear".

23 EXT. EDGEWATER PARK - CAROUSEL 50'S - DAY 23

Another splice and we see BOBBIE and his brother PAUL in front of the carousel. Paul is holding a stuffed animal almost as big as he is.

> BOB
> Oh look, there's me and my brother Paul again. I'm the taller one. He's got four inches on me now.
> (MORE)

(CONTINUED)

23 CONTINUED: 23

                    BOB (cont'd)
          Paul used to be a school teacher.
          Social Studies. He works for my
          father now. A junk dealer. We
          don't talk much anymore. I'm not
          sure you need to know about that.
          You'll learn about life soon enough.

24 INT. JONES BEDROOM - DAY   24

    Film leader and another home movie flickers before us.
    Unexpectedly the projector goes off. BOB steps
    uncomfortably in front of the video camera.

                    BOB
          I can't do this. I hate home
          movies. I never liked other
          people's. I never liked my own.
          Look, I'm sorry. Making videos
          isn't my calling. I should hire
          somebody else.

25 OMIT   25

26 INT. TAN CAR - DAY   26

    BOB and GAIL are sitting in a large BMW sedan driving down
    San Vicente Boulevard. BOB is talking on the car phone.
    GAIL is driving.

                    BOB
          Just tell Arnie I got Cynthia a
          spot on the Today Show. They'll
          tape her at home on Friday. But
          tell her to do some work on her
          kitchen. Rent some groceries or
          something. Right...right. Okay.
          You have any messages for the
          office?
                (GAIL shakes her head
                 "no")
          We'll see you in a few minutes,
          bye.

    He hangs up and reaches down to push a tape into the tape
    deck. Smokey and the Miracles comes blasting out. Gail
    reaches over and turns the music down.

                    GAIL
          Hey. Equal time, huh? Can "we"
          talk a minute? This is important.

                                                        (CONTINUED)

26 CONTINUED:

BOB looks at her.

                  GAIL
              (continuing)
      I spoke with Robin yesterday, about
      that Chinese healer. And don't
      give me that look. He helped her
      father.

                  BOB
      A healer? Gail, for God's sake. I
      may have a tumor but it's not in my
      brain.

GAIL looks hurt.

                  BOB
              (continuing)
      Besides, you know what they say
      about Chinese healers. Half an hour
      after they heal you, you feel like
      you have to be healed again. Forget
      healers.

BOB turns the music back up. GAIL reaches over and turns it off.

                  GAIL
      Bob, listen to me. Stop it. There
      are people out there who want to
      help and you're turning them all
      down. I just think we have to try
      everything.

                  BOB
      I am trying everything. I've been
      to four clinics an three states.
      I've had more second opinions than
      there are doctors. I'm drinking
      macrobiotic sludge for breakfast
      and pumping Laetrile into my body
      on an hourly basis. I am doing
      everything.
              (pause)
      Honey, lookit, eight percent of
      people getting Interleuken-2 have
      total remission. Survival for
      Laetrile patients is around six.
      I figure if you add up all the
      percentages from all the stuff I'm
      taking, I've got about a hundred
      and twenty-two percent chance of
      survival here. So relax okay.
      Don't give up hope on me.

(CONTINUED)

26 CONTINUED: 2   26

>   GAIL
>   Give up hope? I'm living on hope.
>   It's what I breathe.

27 OMIT   27

28 OMIT   28

29 OMIT   29

30 INT. R.A. JONES, PUBLIC RELATIONS - DAY   30

CUT TO PHOTOGRAPHS and other memorabilia lining the shelves of a plush public relations office. We see photos of BOB with Hollywood personalities, sports figures, and several African dignitaries. Magazines are everywhere. We can hear BOB talking in the background.

As the camera pulls back it reveals palm trees and the hills of Los Angeles outside a large picture window. After a moment we see BOB sitting behind a large desk. He is speaking to his assistant, LAURA, who is seated across from him. Three huge rolodexes are positioned on the desk top and colored "post-it" notes are everywhere.

>   BOB
>   After that, tell George to go to
>   Oshmans. Tell him to buy a couple
>   bats, mitts, T-shirts, you know.
>   Send 'em to Randy Spikes with a note
>   saying, "Get your kid into little
>   league. We'll worry about the
>   contract later."
>
>   LAURA
>   That's so sweet.
>
>   BOB
>   I'm a wonderful human being. Okay,
>   next. This is to Steve Elliot. A
>   telegram. "Dear Steve, Fuck you,
>   Love Bob."
>   LAURA
>   Isn't that a little flowery?
>
>   BOB
>   It'll do.

A voice yells out from down the hall.

(CONTINUED)

30   CONTINUED:

> GAIL (O.S.)
> Bob, you got Claude calling on line 2.

> BOB
> (yelling back)
> Claude who?

GAIL sticks her head in the door.

> GAIL
> People Magazine, the new guy.

> BOB
> Oh yeah. Thanks. People Magazine. America's gift to constipation.
> (he picks up the phone with sudden sweetness)
> Claude, how the hell are you?... Great. We're great too. So what's happening with the piece?... You told me you'd get Jennifer a page or two... Whataya mean? She's up for the lead in two films. Everyone wants her. She's happening.
> (pause)
> Okay. Okay. One page.
> (pause)
> Alright, look, I'm getting the distinct impression you don't want to do the piece. It's okay. I understand. I can live with it. Only one thing. Don't come crawling to me when you want do Brando.
> (Laura stares at him)
> What do you mean? Who do you think's promoting his new book?
> (Laura shakes her head)
> Okay, that's better. I thought we could find some agreement here. Just get me two pages and I'll be a happy man. That's great Claude. Talk to you soon.

He hangs up. Laura just stares at him.

> LAURA
> Marlon Brando?

(CONTINUED)

BOB
Marlon? Did I say Marlon? I didn't say Marlon. I just said Brando.

LAURA
You said you'd get him an interview.

BOB
What are you talking about? No I didn't. You weren't listening. I just said don't come crawling to me if he wanted one. I was very careful about that. I'm always very careful. I never lie. If you want to learn this business you have to pay attention.

(CONTINUED)

                    LAURA
          You're amazing. What incredible
          bullshit.

                    BOB
          I wasn't bullshitting.

                    LAURA
          Come on. You said you were
          promoting his new book.

                    BOB
          No I didn't. What's the matter,
          don't you have ears? I was very
          specific. I said "Who do think is
          promoting his book?" "Who?" Did
          you hear me say it was me?

                    LAURA
          Bob, that's immoral.

                    BOB
          It's not immoral. It's P.R.

There is a knock at the door. BOB turns around. GEORGE, an
office boy, is standing there nervously.

                    BOB
          George, come on in.
                    (to Laura)
          Give us a minute, okay?

She nods and walks out. BOB motions for GEORGE to sit as he
pushes a button under his desk and the door closes.

                    BOB
                    (continuing)
          So what's up? Did you finish?

                    GEORGE
          It's not going to work, Mr. Jones.
          It's just not happening, you know.
          I mean, maybe I'm not the person to
          do this.

                    BOB
          What are you talking about? I
          thought you wanted to be a
          filmmaker. This is your chance.

                                             (CONTINUED)

30 CONTINUED: 3   30

                    GEORGE
          I know. I'm sorry. Maybe you need
          a professional, someone who knows
          how to open people up. I'm not good
          at that.

                    BOB
          Sure you are. You got the tape?

                    GEORGE
                (hesitating)
          Well...yeah, but it's no good. I
          don't think you want to see it.

                    BOB
          Let me look.

31 INT. R.A.JONES, PUBLIC RELATIONS - DAY   31

On a video monitor DOROTHY, a dowdy looking woman, stares
uncomfortably into the lens. She seems nervous.

                    DOROTHY
          What does he want?

                    GEORGE (O.S.)
          Just a few words, things you
          remember about him. Funny moments,
          things like that.

                    DOROTHY
          Funny moments? What's he talking
          about? What's he want this for?

                    GEORGE (O.S.)
          I don't know exactly. I think it's
          some kind of a surprise. He doesn't
          want Gail to know.

                    DOROTHY
          Has anyone else done it?

                    GEORGE (O.S.)
          Brenda.

                    DOROTHY
          What did she say?

                    GEORGE (O.S.)
          Not much. She just kind of sat
          there. I had to erase it.

                    DOROTHY
          Great. Look, why don't you try
          someone else first. Okay?

32 INT. R.A.JONES, PUBLIC RELATIONS - SAM'S OFFICE - DAY 32

SAM WALSHSTEADER, a heavyset man, sits behind a desk.

                    SAM
          Bob Jones is one of the great men
          in public relations. L.A. Magazine
          rated him one of the top ten most
          powerful men in the field. He's
          charming, funny, clever. A wheeler
          dealer. I've watched him build
          this business from nothing. Last
          year we were the eighth highest
          grossing P.R. firm in L.A.

                    GEORGE (O.S.)
          What about personal stuff?

                    SAM
          Personal?

                    GEORGE (O.S.)
          Whatever you talk about outside the
          office.

SAM just sits there. The answer eludes him. BOB, watching
the tape, calls out.

                    BOB
          Hey, come on. Sports. Movies.

                    SAM
          He loves the Raiders.

                    BOB
          Yeah!

                    GEORGE (O.S.)
          Isn't there anything else?

                    SAM
          Not really. He's a business man.
          P.R. is his life.

33 INT. R.A.JONES, PUBLIC RELATIONS - DAY 33

DEBORAH LOWENSTEIN, an attractive blonde, peers at her
reflection in the camera lens.

                    DEBORAH
          How's my hair? I look okay? Okay.
          I've known Mr. Jones for five
          months and he's the best boss I've
          ever had, ever, in my entire life.
                    (MORE)

                                              (CONTINUED)

33 CONTINUED:

>   DEBORAH(cont'd)
>   He never complains when I give him
>   the wrong phone message, or
>   disconnect him, or lose a call.
>   He's very compassionate. I really
>   think he's great.

BOB nods as if to say "smart girl".

>   DEBORAH
>   (continuing)
>   That the kind of stuff you want?

34 INT. R.A.JONES, PUBLIC RELATIONS - DAY

CUT TO WALTER SHAYE, a balding executive.

>   WALTER
>   You sure it's off?

>   GEORGE (O.S.)
>   I'm not even touching it.

Suddenly we hear GEORGE say, "Oh shit," as he jumps up to turn off the tape.

>   GEORGE
>   I didn't know that recorded.

>   BOB
>   Wait!

He wants to watch. The video continues.

>   WALTER
>   The truth is I don't really know
>   him. I don't know if anybody knows
>   him, including himself. His is not
>   what you call an examined life.
>   Why does he want you to make this
>   anyway? Is he throwing a
>   testimonial dinner for himself?

>   GEORGE (O.S.)
>   I don't know.

>   WALTER
>   God, this is tricky. I mean, the
>   truth is, he's mostly a product of
>   his own P.R.

>   GEORGE
>   What do you mean?

(CONTINUED)

34   CONTINUED: 34

                        WALTER
        I mean...like his MBA. He tells
        everyone he went to the University
        of Michigan. In fact he graduated
        from Wayne State and only went to
        Michigan for one semester. He's
        brilliant with resumes. You want
        to know something really
        interesting? His name's not even
        Jones. It's Ivanovich or
        something.
            (looking at the camera)
        Why's that red light on?

                        GEORGE
        I think it just means the battery's
        charged.

                        WALTER
        Ahh.

                        GEORGE (O.S.)
        This is horrible. Is there
        <u>anything</u> nice you can say?

                        WALTER
        Boy, you're really putting me to
        the test here. Yeah, I can make
        something up. I'm a P.R. man.
        Turn it on. I'll tell you about
        his charity work. He'll like that.

                        GEORGE (O.S.)
        Okay. I'm ready. Rolling.

The screen goes blank.

35   INT. R.A.JONES, PUBLIC RELATIONS - BOB'S OFFICE - DAY   35

BOB is sitting in the office opposite GEORGE as the tape
ends. GEORGE is red faced.

                        GEORGE
        I didn't know that recorded.

BOB doesn't say a word. Suddenly the Oprah Winfrey Show
comes blaring into the room. BOB points the remote control
at the T.V. and turns it off. For a moment he stares
absently out the window and then turns to GEORGE.

                        BOB
        Okay. Just leave the tape.

                                          (CONTINUED)

| 35 | CONTINUED: | 35 |

>   GEORGE
>   I'm really sorry Mr. Jones.

BOB doesn't answer. GEORGE leaves the room.

| 36 | INT. VERSAILLES RESTAURANT - NIGHT | 36 |

Plates of chicken, rice, beans, and fried plantains lead the camera to a table just past BOB and GAIL in a funky Cuban restaurant. BOB looks over at the food and shakes his head. He seems agitated. He turns back to the menu.

>   GAIL
>   Dr. Califano's office called. They
>   want to see us on Friday. Test
>   results. You listening?
>
>   BOB
>   (he's not)
>   I can't eat any of this.
>
>   GAIL
>   (shaking her head)
>   How about some plain chicken? We
>   can ask them to boil it.
>
>   BOB
>   You want me to vomit all over the
>   table? I'm telling you, I can't
>   eat.
>
>   GAIL
>   Some plain rice maybe? That
>   shouldn't upset...
>
>   BOB
>   Listen, forget it. Just order what
>   you want.
>
>   GAIL
>   Maybe we should leave.
>
>   BOB
>   Get off it, Gail. We didn't come
>   here for me. You've been craving
>   Cuban for a week.

They sit silently for a moment.

>   GAIL
>   I need to tell you something else.
>   I'm having another ultrasound.
>   (MORE)

(CONTINUED)

36 CONTINUED:

GAIL
(cont'd)
Not right away. Down the road. I'd like you to be there.
(BOB closes his eyes)
Wait. Before you reject this, just listen. I think it would be good for you. It'll give us a picture of the baby. You'll be able to see it. We might even find out if it's a boy or a girl. We'd be able to choose a name, buy clothes...and I need to share this with you Bob. Don't make me go through it alone. Please. It's our baby.

BOB
What are you doing to me? How many times can we discuss this? I just have to deal with it in my own way.

GAIL
What way? By avoiding the issue every time I bring it up? What kind of dealing is that? It's your child. It needs your love. It's alive, Bob. It moves. It feels. Don't pretend it away.

BOB
I'm not pretending it away. I'm setting up trust funds. I'm taking care of its future. What kind of pretending is that?

BOB turns away. GAIL'S eyes fill with tears.

GAIL
Why are you doing this?
(with empathy)
Damn it. I know. I know why. I'm angry too. There's nothing but anger. I'm angry at God. I'm angry at the universe. But I don't throw it up at you every time I talk, every time I breathe.
(beat)
Oh God, Bob, please...love us.

She starts to cry. BOB sits motionless, his fists tightly clenched. The silence between them is painful.

37 INT. JONES KITCHEN - DAY   37

GAIL, standing near the kitchen sink, is grinding a disgusting health food preparation in the blender. DORIS, her mother, is sitting at the counter. She observes her daughter with great compassion.

                    DORIS
          You're amazing, you know that? I
          don't know where you get it from,
          this saintly quality of yours.

                    GAIL
          Saint?! Ha! It's not like I have
          a choice. I just go from moment to
          moment. If I stopped for a second,
          they'd have to shovel me off the
          floor.

                    DORIS
          I couldn't have done it, I'll tell
          you that.

Suddenly GAIL hears BOB approaching. She motions for DORIS to be quiet and quickly moves to pour the thick blended mixture into a tall glass. BOB enters the kitchen as GAIL holds out his drink. He is surprised to see his mother-in-law, sitting there.

                    BOB
          Doris! How exciting! Green sludge
          and my mother-in-law, together in
          the same room. Does it get any
          better than this?

                    DORIS
          Hiya Bobbie. Morning to you too.

He leans down and give her a kiss.

                    BOB
          What did you do, get up at the
          crack of dawn?

                    DORIS
          Beautiful morning. Just felt like
          a drive. I wanted to visit my
          daughter.

                    BOB
          Oh really? She didn't call to
          tempt you with leftover Cuban
          food?

                    DORIS
          I am too old for temptations, Bob.
          Especially left-overs.

                                                          (CONTINUED)

37 CONTINUED:

He winks, enjoying her quick wittedness so early in the morning. After a moment he lifts his drink into the air and eyes it with displeasure.

                        BOB
       To many such lovely mornings. Down
       the hatch.

                        DORIS
       God, how can you drink that?.

                        BOB
       It's not that bad once you get to
       the chewy center.

DORIS makes a face.

BOB downs the concoction and purposely lets it ooze out the sides of his mouth. DORIS looks away.

                        DORIS
       That's disgusting.

                        BOB
       You don't know from disgusting.
       Here, take a taste.

                        DORIS
         (wrinkling her nose)
       Thanks. Maybe next time.

                        BOB
       There may not be a next time.

DORIS takes BOB'S glass and washes it out in the sink.

                        DORIS
         (to Bob)
       You know, you married a saint.

                        BOB
       I know. It's the balance of
       nature. Between us we're almost a
       normal person.

DORIS smiles.

                        GAIL
         (turning to BOB)
       I called your parents this morning.

                                    (CONTINUED)

BOB
(stopping in his
tracks)
You're kidding. Why'd you do that?

GAIL
Somebody had to. I told them you were having tests. They were grateful to know. You should call them.

BOB
I call them all the time. Just the other day. When was it?

GAIL
Four months ago...when we found out I was pregnant. You didn't say two words.
(back to the tests)
Your mother sounded very concerned.

BOB
Concerned? Look, if she loves me so much, let her get on an airplane and come out and see me.

GAIL
She doesn't love God that much.

DORIS
You should call her.

BOB
Why? We have one conversation. How many times do we need to have it?

DORIS
Be grateful they're there.

BOB
Look, spare me, okay. I spent twenty years fighting to get away from Detroit. I don't need to go back.

GAIL
(changing the subject)
Paul's getting married.

BOB
Paul? You're kidding. To who?

(CONTINUED)

37   CONTINUED: 3

> GAIL
> I don't know. Anya something. Your mom said she was lovely.
>
> BOB
> Anya? Right. Probably someone in "food services" or "sanitation" or something exciting like that.
>
> GAIL
> It's April 21st. I think it might be nice if we went.
>
> BOB
> You mean we're invited?

GAIL rolls her eyes.

> BOB
> (continuing)
> Look, forget it. I'll probably be dead by that time anyway.
>
> GAIL
> Great. Then we'll have the perfect excuse for not showing up.

BOB smiles. GAIL grins.

> GAIL
> (continuing)
> Come on. We haven't been there in four years. Will you think about it?
>
> BOB
> I'll see.
>
> DORIS
> We need family, Bob.
>
> GAIL
> It's true. If it wasn't for my mother, who would I have?

GAIL holds her mother's hand.

> BOB
> You'd have me.

GAIL looks at him oddly. They all understand the irony of what he has said.

38 INT. JONES BEDROOM - DAY

A video image appears on the screen. Slowly the winged-back chair bleeds into focus and we see BOB sitting there.

> BOB
> When I was about four years old my mother told me that dying was like going to sleep and never waking up. Where she got that from I'll never know but, idiot that I was, I believed her. Can you imagine. I used to try and imagine what "forever" was. I couldn't do it. How could you never smell coffee again, never see the sun rise? From that time on I've hated sleeping. For years, every night when I went to bed, I'd struggle to find the perfect position, the one that would be comfortable if I had to lie that way "forever". I'd lie on my back. I'd lie on my side. I still haven't found it. The closest I've come is lying next to your mother. Unfortunately, she won't be coming with me. Too bad, huh. Cause then when St. Peter wonders what I'm doing at the Pearly Gates, I could tell him, "I'm with her."
> (pause)
> It's amazing, you know. Here I am, 36 years old and I still haven't the slightest idea what death is. Nothing anybody's ever said made much sense to me. If I've got some kind of immortal soul, then somebody better prove it quick. I've never bought anything on faith.

There is a knock at the door. BOB clutches. We hear a voice on the other side

> DOR@S (V.O.)
> Robert? It's Doris. Are you on the phone? I have your lunch. Who are you talking to? The door's locked. Can I come in?

BOB rolls his eyes. The screen goes blank.

39 EXT. JONES' HOUSE - DAY

BOB'S car pulls out of the driveway and circles around the block.

40   EXT. BOB'S CAR - DAY   40

He finds an empty parking space on a nice, tree lined
street, and pulls into it.

41   INT. BOB'S CAR - DAY   41

BOB sets up the video camera on the dashboard by propping
the Thomas Guide underneath it. He aims it at himself.
Satisfied that it is working, he pushes the remote control
button and starts recording.

CUT TO BOB talking into the camera.

                         BOB
               Rock and roll. That's a very
               important subject. Don't get
               caught up in this heavy metal
               stuff. You gotta know the
               classics. James Brown, the Stones,
               Elvis. And your mother will be
               useless in this. She'll fill your
               head with show tunes. Watch out.
               If she ever starts,
                    (he sings)
               "Some enchanted evening, you will
               meet a stranger"...run as fast as
               you can or you'll have South
               Pacific until it's coming out of
               your nostrils. Believe me. Just
               tell her you want the Temptations.
               Temptations. Can you say that?

BOB is suddenly aware that a police car has pulled up
alongside him and a POLICEMAN is staring curiously at him
through the window. BOB glares back at him and the police
car gradually pulls away. After a moment BOB returns to the
camera but now he feels awkward.

                         BOB
                      (continuing)
               Shit. They ruined the flow.

He grabs for the remote. The screen goes black.

42   INT. CALIFANO'S OFFICE - DAY   42

BOB and GAIL are sitting opposite DR. THOMAS CALIFANO in a
somber doctor's office. DR. CALIFANO does not look happy.
GAIL examines every gesture for hints of what's to come. He
pulls out a file and lays it on the desk.

                                                        (CONTINUED)

42   CONTINUED:

>   CALIFANO
> We got the lab reports back this
> morning. I'm sorry Bob, but they
> don't look good. There has been no
> reduction in tumor size or density.

BOB'S face drops to the floor.

>   CALIFANO
>   (continuing)
> Based on your response to the
> Interleuken therapy, I do not
> recommend further treatment.

>   BOB
> What do you mean?

>   CALIFANO
> I don't believe you could survive
> another course. We're losing
> ground, Bob. The tumor is growing.
> I think you need to accept things
> as they are. We'll continue to
> monitor everything. You could
> still have three or four months. I
> think you should aim for that.

>   BOB
> Four months?

>   CALIFANO
> You've got Spring to look forward
> to. Your health won't be too bad.
> We have drugs to manage the pain.

>   BOB
> But...what if I want to do the
> therapy again, if I elect to do it.
> Will you prevent me? Will you get a
> court order or something?

>   CALIFANO
> I can't believe you're asking this.
> I mean, the Interleuken nearly
> killed you. It was touch and go
> for six hours there and in the end
> it didn't work. Under the
> circumstances, Bob, I can't
> recommend...

>   BOB
> Screw your recommendation! Will
> you let me do it? Are you going to
> interfere with my doing it?

(CONTINUED)

42   CONTINUED: 2   42

                         CALIFANO
               I'm sorry.

                         BOB
               Look, one more treatment. Just
               one. Three strikes and you're out,
               right?

                         CALIFANO
               This isn't baseball you're playing.

                         BOB
               Come on. The game's still alive
               here. There are lots of other
               treatments...therapies.

                         CALIFANO
               Bob, don't make this more painful
               than it has to be. There's not a
               lot of time left. Don't waste it
               in futile searches.
                         (pause)
               Look, medicine has terrible
               limitations. I know you're angry,
               and rightly so. No one's ever
               prepared to deal with this. We can
               put you in touch with support
               groups. I know a great
               psychiatrist. I wish there was
               something else I could say.
                         (beat)
               There aren't any words.

     He reaches out and places his hand on BOB'S shoulder. BOB
     pulls away.

43   EXT. MEDICAL COMPLEX - DAY   43

     BOB and GAIL are walking silently to the car. BOB is about
     to get in when, unexpectedly, he stops. There is an angry
     look on his face. Suddenly, without warning, he turns
     around and storms back toward the clinic. GAIL stares after
     him, confused.

44   INT. CLINIC - DAY   44

     BOB walks down the corridor with a quick and powerful
     stride.

45   INT. DOCTOR'S OFFICE - DAY

BOB slams open the door to DR. CALIFANO'S waiting room and heads straight for his office. The nurses try to hold him back but he is unstoppable. DR. CALIFANO is with a patient. BOB explodes through the door.

> BOB
> How dare you take away my hope! Who the hell do you think you are? You have no right to take that away. You understand me? It's all I have. It's <u>all</u> I have.

THE DOCTOR and his patient just stare in disbelief as BOB walks furiously out of the room. GAIL is standing there, observing him in amazement. BOB rushes past her toward the waiting room. After a moment he turns back and grabs her by the hand. They exit together.

46   INT. JONES BEDROOM - NIGHT

BOB and GAIL are lying apart in their bed staring at the ceiling.

> BOB
> What do we do?

> GAIL
> I don't know anymore. We go on, I suppose.

> BOB
> How?

> GAIL
> We'll figure it out.

There is a long pause. GAIL moves closer to BOB.

> BOB
> I'm gonna beat this thing. I'm gonna beat it, Gail.

> GAIL
> ...I know.

GAIL lays her face gently alongside BOB'S. THE CAMERA MOVES IN CLOSE TO THEM. The expression on both their faces betrays their calm words. We see only fear.

47   OMIT

48   OMIT

49 INT. MR. HO'S OLD BUILDING - HALLWAY & STAIRWELL - DAY

BOB and GAIL are walking up the stairs of a decaying apartment building near downtown L.A.

> BOB
> This is crazy. Look at this place. What if we get hit by a wrecking ball?

> GAIL
> Just close your eyes.

> BOB
> Let's go home.

> GAIL
> We're not going anywhere. Robin's father had pancreatic cancer and now he doesn't. That's all I need to know.

> BOB
> How can they fix bodies if they can't fix hallways?

> GAIL
> That's what we're going to find out.

50 INT. MR. HO'S WAITING ROOM - DAY

BOB and GAIL enter a decrepit room filled with waiting patients. Most are elderly and Chinese. A bare light bulb hangs from the center of the ceiling.

> BOB
> Nice lighting.

They sit on a wooden bench. BOB looks at the people around him and then leans into GAIL and sings.

> BOB
> "One of these things doesn't belong here..."

GAIL hands him a magazine.

> GAIL
> Here, read something.

She hands him a magazine. It's in Chinese. He turns it upside down.

(CONTINUED)

50 CONTINUED: 50

We observe the stack of magazines getting higher as the
waiting room empties out. Suddenly we hear a voice from the
next room calling out.

                    MR. HO (O.S.)
          Mister Jones!

BOB looks up at GAIL apprehensively, hugs her goodbye, and
then crosses to the door.

51 INT. MR. HO'S TREATMENT ROOM - DAY   51

BOB enters a room with many windows, the shabby walls
painted a cheesy off-white.

A single table stands in the middle of the room. A voice
calls out from an open door.

                    MR. HO (O.S.)
          Take off your shoes and lie down.

BOB furrows his brow in dismay but does what he is told.
Slipping off his shoes, he lies down on the table. His eyes
roam around the room and out the windows to bizarre murals
on the buildings across the way. Moments later MR. HO, A
CHINESE HEALER, enters the room. Our first glimpse of him
is of his feet, a pair of old tennis shoes. THE CAMERA
TILTS UP, revealing a small man in a plaid shirt. He seems
quiet and unassuming. There is, however, a strange and
potent energy emanating from him that seems totally at odds
with his appearance. There is no greeting. MR. HO begins
by lifting BOB'S hand and smelling his wrist and checking
various pulse points. BOB is amused by this.

                    BOB
          Just so you know. I'm looking for
          a miracle here.

                    MR. HO
          You believe in miracles?

                    BOB
          I will if this works.

Even before MR. HO reaches BOB he makes his first
pronouncement.

                    MR. HO
          Oh, very bad stomach. You take too
          much Rolaids.

Bob is amazed.

                                                            (CONTINUED)

51 CONTINUED:
51

> BOB
> Yeah, I do. How'd you know that?

He picks up a roll lying beside BOB and shows it to him.

> MR. HO
> It fell out of your pocket. It's half empty.

MR. HO takes BOB'S hand and quickly checks various pulse points on the wrist. Then he lifts the wrist to his nose and begins to smell it. BOB is amused by this. Moving within inches of BOB'S face, MR. HO examines BOB'S left eye. He seems momentarily intrigued.

> MR. HO
> You had your appendix out. A long time ago. You were a child, yes?
> (he peers more closely into the eye)
> Four or five.

> BOB
> Five.

> MR. HO
> Five. That's what I thought.

BOB eyes him with amazement. MR. HO smiles to himself. Quickly, and perfunctorily, he begins to move his hands over BOB'S body, starting at his head. The hands appear to vibrate at varying frequencies. His pointing finger operates like a dowsing rod pointing at problem areas. He is all business.

> MR. HO
> (continuing)
> Ah. The tumors are here, in the lungs. Two of them. Very big.

BOB is astounded. MR. HO'S hands move slowly down to BOB's waist.

> MR. HO
> The disease comes from the kidneys. Very sick. You just get comfortable. I work.

MR. HO holds his right hand lightly over BOB'S left kidney. BOB is hardly aware of him. Instead he is aware of a large standing fan pivoting back and forth across the room. Curtains billow in its wake. Pigeons flutter past the windows. Light patterns from street traffic pass over the walls.

(CONTINUED)

51 CONTINUED: 2

There is a strangeness in the atmosphere, something otherworldly.

The ceiling is made of acoustic tiles with tiny holes. Many are stained with water damage. Suddenly BOB'S vision seems to be rising up to the tiles as the holes draw nearer like so many stars. Unexpectedly, the holes begin to glow.

52 EXT. FOREST - DAY

A BURST OF LIGHT. The camera glides through a bamboo forest. Sunlight filters magically through the tall reeds. A canopy of pastoral greenery shimmers before us, primordial in its beauty. We can see a YOUNG MAN, backlit, walking toward us. He is strong and beautiful. The camera approaches him slowly and stops. We hear BOB'S voice.

>BOB (V.O.)
>Where am I? Who are you?

The YOUNG MAN speaks with unexpected depth.

>MAN
>Name me.

53 INT. MR. HO'S TREATMENT ROOM - DAY

There is a sudden flash of blinding light and BOB'S body lurches upward in the healer's office. He seems totally confused. MR. HO continues as though nothing has happened.

>MR. HO
>You must relax.

>BOB
>I'm trying. What was that? That hurt.

>MR. HO
>Healing can be a painful process.

>BOB
>No kidding.

MR. HO tries gently to lower BOB back onto the table but he refuses to lie back down.

>MR. HO
>You fight me. You make it hard for me to do. You hold too much anger inside. It poisons you.
>(MORE)

(CONTINUED)

53 CONTINUED:
53

> MR. HO (CONT'D)
> I try to take the poison away but you won't let it go. Why do you hang onto your anger so much?

> BOB
> (annoyed)
> I'm not hanging on to anything.

BOB gets off the table, walks over to a small stool, and begins putting on his shoes. MR. HO comes over to him.

> MR. HO
> Do you want to carry so much pain into your next life?

> BOB
> Next life? Whataya mean, "next" life?

MR. HO pauses a second and then leans down toward BOB. He speaks with hushed tones, his voice full of power.

> MR. HO
> The last second of your life is the most important moment of all. It is everything you are...ever said...ever thought... all rolled into one. That is the seed of your next life. Until that last moment, you still have time...you can change...everything. You can let go of your fear, let go of your anger.

BOB stands up, his shoe laces still untied.

> BOB
> I'm not angry!

> MR. HO
> So I see.

54 OMIT
54

54A EXT. DOWNTOWN STREET - DAY
54A

BOB and GAIL are leaving MR. HO'S office. BOB seems angry.

> BOB
> A quack. A total charlatan quack.

(CONTINUED)

54A CONTINUED: 54A

                    GAIL
          You didn't feel anything?

                    BOB
          Just the urge to get out. He kept
          telling me how angry I was, the
          stupid son-of-a-bitch. Shit!

                    GAIL
          What else did he say?

                    BOB
          He went on and on. He said I had
          no faith. He said life was trying
          to talk to me all the time. That
          it's sending me invitations. What
          invitations has life sent me? Huh?
          That's what I'd like to know.

                    GAIL
          You got one to your brother's
          wedding.

                    BOB
          I don't think that's what he meant.

55   INT. GYM - DAY   55

BOB and his associate ARNOLD SHERMAN are playing
racquetball. BOB is playing with a vengeance, pushing
himself to the limit. It is scary to watch him. With one
misguided swing he nearly kills ARNOLD.

                    ARNOLD
          Hey, chill out. It's just a game.

56   INT. SAUNA - DAY   56

A spray of water hits a pile of heated rocks in a fancy
gymnasium sauna. A blast of steam surges into the room.
The camera follows the steam upward and reveals BOB and
ARNOLD sitting at different heights on the hardwood benches.

                    ARNOLD
          Reincarnation?

ARNOLD sprinkles more water from a plastic water bottle onto
the rocks. There is more steam. Both men have broken out
in a heavy sweat.

                    BOB
          I just want to know if you believe
          in it?

                                                      (CONTINUED)

56 CONTINUED:

ARNOLD
I don't know. If you put it on the ballot, I'd vote for it, okay. Why?

BOB
I don't know. It's just, lately, I've been thinking about it.

ARNOLD
Thinking about it? What's to think about? Bob, you're making two fifty a year. You're in the top one percentile. Stop contemplating the afterlife and enjoy this one.

BOB
But don't you ever wonder what it's all about...? why you're here...? who you really are...?

ARNOLD
No.
    (pause)
What is it with you? You're a philosopher all of a sudden? I took philosophy in college. It never got me anywhere.

BOB
Are you happy?

ARNOLD
    (getting uncomfortable)
Bobbie, boy, get off it.

BOB
I'm serious. When was the last time you were honestly happy?

ARNOLD
I was happy beating you at handball. I've been happy taking this sauna. In fact I've been happy with everything up until this conversation. Are you feeling okay?

BOB
    (suddenly paranoid)
Whataya mean? Why?

(CONTINUED)

56 CONTINUED: 2   56

                    ARNOLD
          Cause you're just getting weird in
          your old age. Stop tormenting
          yourself so much. Turn it off.

He raises his hand and snaps his fingers.

THE SCREEN GOES BLACK.

57 EXT. HOLLYWOOD HOME - DAY   57

A video image fills the screen. We are approaching a small
house in the Hollywood Hills. We see a hand reach out and
ring the doorbell. After a moment a middle aged WOMAN
appears. She stares at the camera curiously.

                    CAROL
          Hello.

                    BOB (V.O.)
          Carol? Carol Sandman?

                    CAROL
               (surprised)
          Sandman? That was years ago. Who
          are you? What's the camera?

                    BOB (V.O.)
          I'm Bob...Bobbie Ivanovich.

                    CAROL
          Bobbie?
               (she stares at him)
          On my God. I don't believe this.
          Bobbie! What are you doing here?
          How did you find me?

                    BOB (V.O.)
          I ran into Tony Farantino a while
          back. He told me you were living
          here.

                    CAROL
          Tony! God, this is amazing. It's
          gotta be twenty-five, thirty years.
          Look at you! You've grown up. This
          is great. Oh God, I'm so excited.
          Hey, come on in.

58 INT. HOLLYWOOD HOME - DAY   58

The video camera sits on a small tripod on CAROL'S coffee
table. It is focused on her sitting on the couch and
records her as she talks.

                                                      (CONTINUED)

58 CONTINUED:

CAROL
That's so amazing. How can you not remember? You lived right next door.

BOB
I think I've repressed it all. I sort of remember your parents and your brother a little bit.

CAROL
He's married. He's got three kids.
    (rolling her eyes)
He owns a gun shop in San Antonio.

BOB
You're kidding!

CAROL
I've got two kids myself. Mara's in pre-school and Sophia...you'll hear her. She could wake up any minute.

BOB
That's great. We're about to have our first.

CAROL
Oh Bobbie. It's so exciting. Little Bobbie.

BOB
I'm making this tape for him...her...you know, whoever it turns out to be. Sort of exploring my past, I guess. I want 'im to know something about me. The problem is...I don't remember a lot. I was such a different person back then.

CAROL
Weren't we all?

BOB
Tell me something. Do you remember much about those days?

CAROL
Are you kidding? Of course I do. I really do. You and me, we'd laugh for hours. We used to sit in my bedroom and listen to Petula Clark sing "Downtown" over and over, and you would dance.

(CONTINUED)

58 CONTINUED: 2

> BOB
> I danced?

> CAROL
> You'd spin all around until you fell over, laughing. And we'd play Chutes and Ladders with my brother. And you used to play my accordion. You really don't remember?

> BOB
> Nope. You could be describing Mickey Mantle for all I know.

> CAROL
> You were funny, always making up stories. You used to tell us how your father was a secret FBI agent, remember that? And how you were going to be famous when you grew up. You had these dreams. And now it's so amazing. Look at you, you've made it.

> BOB
> (humbly)
> Well, hardly.

We hear the sound of a baby crying.

> CAROL
> Oh God, here we go.

She jumps up. The camera cuts off.

58A LATER, IN ANOTHER PART OF THE HOUSE

The camera cuts back on and we see BOB holding the baby as CAROL shoots. He seems very uncomfortable.

> CAROL (V.O.)
> (trying to be polite)
> That's good. That looks natural.

> BOB
> I don't feel natural.

> CAROL (V.O.)
> It takes practice. You'll be a great father. I can tell.

> BOB
> What do you know that I don't know.

(CONTINUED)

58A   CONTINUED: 58A

The baby starts to cry. CAROL reaches out to exchange the camera for the baby. Now BOB aims at her.

                    CAROL
                   (continuing)
You know what my Uncle Rudi always said? The best thing parents can do for their children is to love each other. Kids have to marinate in love, he said. Sixteen years and they're really juicy.

                    BOB (V.O.)
That's great. I knew I needed to see you for something.

                    CAROL
Seek and ye shall find.

                    BOB(V.O.)
I've never been much of a seeker.

                    CAROL
What do you mean? You found me, didn't you?

BOB laughs.

                    BOB (V.O.)
It's great to be here Carol.

                    CAROL
It really is.

The camera turns off.

59   INT. JONES BEDROOM - DAY   59

We see BOB through the video lens. He is sitting alone on top of a large hill.

A vast expanse of hills rolls off in the distance. They all look parched, a dusty California brown. BOB is talking to the camera.

                    BOB
This is a delicate subject. Someday Mom may want to get married again and you may feel a little strange about that. You may even be a little angry, like maybe she's being disloyal to me. Well, let's think this over.

                                          (CONTINUED)

59 CONTINUED: 59

THE CAMERA BEGINS TO PULL BACK and we realize that we are watching a tape on the bedroom monitor.

> BOB
> (continuing)
> Your mother's a pretty wonderful person. I mean, she married me, didn't she? But she may be lonely. Did you think of that?

THE CAMERA CONTINUES TO PULL BACK and we are gradually aware that it is GAIL, sitting there, watching the tape.

> BOB
> (continuing)
> And what if this guy's nice and you really like him? That'd be great, huh? He could play baseball with you and take you to the Lakers. And don't worry that I'd be jealous - well, maybe a little, since he'd be doing all those things that I wanted to do...

Quietly the door to the bedroom opens and BOB peers in. He is carrying a load of packages.

He is stunned to see that GAIL is watching his tape.

> BOB
> What the hell? Where'd you find...? Who said you could play those tapes?

GAIL holds up her hand to quiet him and continues listening. BOB just stands there uncomfortably, his privacy invaded, his secret discovered.

> BOB
> (continuing)
> But if he's smart, he'll never try to take my place because you and I know that I'm your "dad" and that's forever. I'm not saying this is absolutely going to happen, but if it does, I wanted you to know how I feel. We both want your mom to be happy, don't we?

BOB walks over to the camera and turns it off. He pushes the eject button, removes the tape, and places it in the bottom drawer of the cabinet under the television. Other tapes are already lying there. GAIL looks up at him with tears running down her cheeks.

> GAIL
> Why didn't you tell me?

CONTINUED: 2

He is guilty, embarrassed.

                    BOB
          I couldn't.

                    GAIL
          I wish I could tell you that I love
          it, that I admire what you've done,
          but mostly...it hurts me Bob.
          Maybe it shouldn't, but it does.
                (she is all choked up)
          Why don't you ever tell me these
          things? Why is it you can tell all
          this to a camera, that you can open
          your heart to a machine? I'm flesh
          and blood.
                (she cries)
          I ache so much. I don't know if I
          can make it from day to day. Your
          silence doesn't protect me, Bob.
          I'm drowning in it.
                (pause)
          A machine. It's not fair.
          Nothing's fair. I feel like I've
          already lost you, like we've lost
          each other.

                    BOB
          Gail, please. Listen to me. Let
          me talk...

                    GAIL
          No. Don't charm me out of this.
          Don't give me your P.R. shit.

                    BOB
          What do you want me to say?

                    GAIL
          Don't say anything. Just hear me
          for once. Feel my pain. I need
          you too, Bob. I can't do this
          alone. I need you to be there.

                    BOB
          What? How can I be there?

                    GAIL
          I don't know. Open your heart.
          Let me inside. Share what you're
          feeling.

BOB stands there, not knowing what to say. GAIL, her heart
aching, turns and walks out of the room. BOB is left alone.

60   EXT. DARK FIELD - NIGHT   60

ALL IS DARKNESS. Far in the distance a man is heard, asking for breath. It takes a moment to recognize that it is BOB running toward us furiously. Something is pursuing him. There is terror in his face. We hear the sound of hooves and animals growling. Dark forces are gaining on him. He stumbles and scrambles back to his feet. The sounds close in. Suddenly we hear a terrifying scream.

61   INT. JONES BEDROOM - NIGHT   61

GAIL quickly turns on the light and sees BOB sitting up in bed. He is gasping for breath, totally disoriented. She reaches out and grabs hold of him.

                    GAIL
Bob, you're all right. It's okay. I'm here.

                    BOB
I don't want to die. Don't let me die.

                    GAIL
It's all right.

                    BOB
I want to live.

                    GAIL
I know.

                    BOB
I want to live.

62   INT. MR. HO'S TREATMENT ROOM - LATE AFTERNOON   62

Starting with a shot of MR. HO'S right hand on the sole of BOB'S foot, the camera begins a long tracking shot moving along BOB'S entire body and coming to rest on his head. Gradually we see that MR. HO is also touching BOB'S heart and seems to be sending a current of energy through his chest to his feet. During this strange healing operation MR. HO is talking.

                    MR. HO
If you want to know the truth, I'm surprised you came back.

                    BOB
Me too.

(CONTINUED)

62 CONTINUED:

> MR. HO
> Most people like you come once and I
> don't see them again.

> BOB
> It was my wife's idea.

> MR. HO
> She's a very good woman.

> BOB
> I know. Very good. That's why I
> married her.

> MR. HO
> It's not enough to marry goodness.
> You have to find it in yourself.
>   (beat)
> Try and relax.

> BOB
>   (tense)
> I am relaxed.

MR. HO shakes his head. He works on BOB'S body for a few moments. Like the last time there is a sudden flash of light.

63 EXT. FIELD - LATE AFTERNOON

CUT TO A HUGE TREE. The same young man we saw before is standing beneath it. He walks gently toward the camera and pauses just in front of it. Quietly, openly, he speaks.

> MAN
> Surrender.

64 INT. MR. HO'S TREATMENT ROOM - LATE AFTERNOON

There is another bolt of light and BOB shoots upright.

> BOB
> God. What are you doing to me?

> MR. HO
> That was good. I got some poison
> out. Now I can see more clearly.

MR. HO begins moving his hand over BOB'S back as BOB sits there mystified and confused by what is happening.

(CONTINUED)

64 CONTINUED:

> MR. HO
> (continuing)
> Your anger is very deep, very old.

> BOB
> Who've you been talking to? My wife?

> MR. HO
> Don't be afraid to let go. Free yourself of your anger or you will find no peace.

> BOB
> And how do you propose I do that?

> MR. HO
> You start with forgiveness. Forgive those who hurt you. Forgive yourself.

MR. HO moves his right hand gently over BOB'S head and then places it on BOB'S chest. His left hand remains on BOB'S back. It is as though he is sending energy right through the body.

> BOB
> You have been talking to her!

> MR. HO
> I talk to nobody. I listen to your heart. If you listened to it, you would not need me. Your heart is crying out... "forgive".

> BOB
> Forgive who? I don't have to forgive anybody.

> MR. HO
> Okay. That's your choice.

65 INT. AIRPLANE - DAY

A majestic image of a cloud-filled sky fills the screen. It takes a moment to realize that it is on video.

> BOB (V.O.)
> Here we are, blue skies, white clouds, winging our way over the majestic Rockies on our way to picturesque Detroit.
> (MORE)

(CONTINUED)

65 CONTINUED:

>   BOB (V.O.) (cont'd)
>   You want to know why we're making
>   this epic, two thousand mile
>   journey? Well let me put on someone
>   who can tell you.

The camera pulls back from the airplane window and reveals GAIL sitting beside it. She smiles.

>   BOB (V.O.)
>   (continuing)
>   Okay, Mom, tell your child why we
>   are going to the one place on earth
>   I tried hardest to get away from.
>
>   GAIL
>   Because your Uncle Paul is getting
>   married and they invited us to
>   come. Because this video wouldn't
>   be complete without showing where
>   your father used to live. Because
>   your father needs to see his
>   family. You want more?

BOB turns the camera on himself.

>   BOB
>   See?

66 INT. HOTEL ROOM - DAY

BOB'S video camera is roaming through a Ramada Inn hotel room in suburban Detroit. He is pretending to be a cameraman for a live police docudrama like "Top Cops".

The camera roams through a medicine cabinet, over hotel dressers, and into GAIL'S purse. Ultimately we find GAIL asleep, lying on the bed, her feet propped on several pillows.

>   BOB (V.O.)
>   (whispering)
>   Okay, here we are with the Detroit
>   Police department in a secret raid
>   on a hotel room in suburban drug
>   infested Detroit. Somewhere in
>   this room is a major drug supply,
>   aspirin with codeine, Alka Seltzer
>   Plus, and other nefarious
>   pharmaceutical products. Ah ha.
>   There's the suspect over on the
>   bed. We are now going under the
>   covers. This is a true undercover
>   operation.
>   (MORE)

(CONTINUED)

CONTINUED:

> BOB (V.O.) (cont'd)
> Ah ha. These are the lovely legs of our suspect. No. This is police work. We're not supposed to look at lovely legs. But they are nice legs. Oh my God, she's pregnant. Okay we're ready to make an arrest. Lady, you're under arrest.

> GAIL
> Bob, what the hell are you doing?

(CONTINUED)

66 CONTINUED:

>   BOB (V.O.)
>   Wait. She's up. And her eyes are
>   dilated. Yes, she's guilty.
>   Guilty. And half naked.
>
>   GAIL
>   Come on. Go shoot something
>   useful. I need to rest.

BOB puts down the camera and reaches into her purse for the car keys.

>   BOB
>   Do you mind? I'll be back in an
>   hour.
>
>   GAIL
>   Just drive carefully. You take
>   your pills?
>
>   BOB
>   Fully medicated.

He kisses her feet, turns and walks into a wall. She laughs. He smiles.

>   BOB
>   (continuing)
>   Just kidding. See you soon.

67 OMIT

68 OMIT

68A EXT. RESIDENTIAL NEIGHBORHOOD - DAY

BOB'S car rides slowly down familiar tree lined streets we saw at the opening of the film. The houses are still mostly small, 1950's vintage, but they have much more extensive vegetation now. Some have chain link fences.

>   BOB (V.O.)
>   This is the old neighborhood where I
>   grew up. I was going to show you
>   all the places I used to go, the
>   grocery store, the shoe store I
>   worked in. Unfortunately they've
>   all been torn down, paved over.

He turns the camera on himself.

(CONTINUED)

68A CONTINUED: 68A

                    BOB
                 (continuing)
         It's odd, you know, all the places
         I remember most...covered in
         cement. My whole life...one big
         parking lot.

69 EXT. JAMES VERNOR SCHOOL - DAY 69

    BOB is roaming around an empty school yard.

                    BOB (V.O.)
         This is the James Vernor Elementary
         School. I spent eight years here.
         See that alley way? I got the shit
         kicked out of me right in that
         corner. Eric Dunsforth called me a
         Pollack. I said I was Ukrainian.
         It didn't seem to matter. He
         creamed me anyway. I was never
         much of a fighter. Until I fought
         to get out of Detroit. That I
         fought for. Everything in Detroit
         was about failure to me. My father
         was a failure, I was a failure...or
         I was afraid of becoming one. In
         Los Angeles I became my own person.
         I left everything else behind.

70 OMIT 70

70A EXT. FORMER IVANOVICH HOUSE - DAY 70A

    BOB pulls up in front of an old house. We recognize it. It
    was his home.

71 EXT. IVANOVICH FORMER HOUSE - DAY 71

    Hesitantly, BOB rings the doorbell. No one answers. He
    knocks. No response. Not sure what to do, he steps off the
    porch and walks slowly around to the backyard gate. He
    looks into the yard. There is no one home.

    BOB unlocks the gate.

72 EXT. IVANOVICH FORMER HOUSE - BACKYARD - DAY 72

    BOB enters the backyard. It is still recognizable from the
    beginning of the film, the same one-car garage, the tiny
    patch of grass.

                                                  (CONTINUED)

72 CONTINUED:

It is obvious from the expression on BOB'S face that the yard holds many vague memories for him. We experience his conflicting sense of ownership and strangeness.

Far in the distance we hear children's voice. It is hard to tell if it is the sound of kids playing nearby or of his own past rising up in his mind.

                    BOB
                 (to himself)
        This used to be so big.

Suddenly there is a glimmer in his eyes and an odd smiles on his face.

CUT TO A CINDER BLOCK in a low corner wall of the house. BOB'S hands surrounds it easily. With a firm tug he yanks it forward. He is delighted to see that it is still loose. Edging it out he reaches into its hollow core and slowly, almost magically, extracts a thirty years old GI JOE FIGURE with a parachute attached. BOB is thrilled to see it. With an exuberant and childlike glee, he tosses it up into the sky.

The chute opens and he watches as it floats back down to earth.

A shrill scream fills the air and nearly knocks BOB off his feet.

                  LITTLE GIRL
    Mommy! Mommy!

Heart pounding, BOB looks up and sees a little BLACK GIRL entering the backyard gate through BOB'S swinging slat. Almost instantly her MOTHER appears, carrying two bags of groceries. She gasps.

                  WOMAN
        Oh my God...!

There is a look of fear and confusion on her face as she sees BOB kneeling by the side of her house. He jumps to his feet and tries to explain.

                    BOB
        It's okay. It's okay. I'm Bob
        Jones. Ivanovich. I lived here.
        I used to live here. This was my
        home.

The woman stares at him nervously. He tries to smile and assure her with his gestures. THE LITTLE GIRL hides behind her mother's skirt.

                                      (CONTINUED)

72 CONTINUED: 2   72

                              BOB
                         (continuing)
                    It's okay, really.

THE WOMAN nods. We sense that everything will be all right.

73 INT. IVANOVICH FORMER HOUSE - DAY   73

BOB moves silently through his childhood house, his camera
dangling at his side.

There is an elegiac sense of continuous movement as he
touches walls, banisters, window sills. It is all familiar
to us from the opening of the film. His memories are ours.
We hear sounds from years before playing in his head.

74 INT. IVANOVICH FORMER HOUSE - STAIRS - DAY   74

BOB walks up the stairs.

75 INT. IVANOVICH FORMER HOUSE - BEDROOM - DAY   75

BOB enters his old bedroom. There is a piece of peeling
wallpaper. He pulls it back and sees through the layers a
design that is familiar to him. The power of it takes him
by surprise. He stares at it lovingly. Suddenly the LITTLE
GIRL appears beside him.

                         LITTLE GIRL
                    (warming up to him)
                    Did you sleep here too?

                         BOB
                    Uh huh. When I was little. About
                    your age.

                         LITTLE GIRL
                    In my bed?

                         BOB
                    No, no. I had my own bed. It was
                    right here. By the window. The
                    Sandmans lived there.

He points to the house across the way.

                         LITTLE GIRL
                    That's the Robinsons. They live
                    there now.

                         BOB
                    My brother slept in a bed over
                    here. We used to talk all night.

                                                              (CONTINUED)

75 CONTINUED:

                    LITTLE GIRL
          I don't have a brother. Mommy said
          Daddy's gonna get me one.

THE LITTLE GIRL smiles.

                    LITTLE GIRL
                      (continuing)
          You wanna see where I hide?

BOB nods. She takes him over to the tiny storage closet cut
into the attic wall.

                    BOB
          I used to hide in there too.

He stoops down, holding his back, and cautiously but
curiously, steps inside. The camera follows him into the
darkness.

76 INT. BOBBIE'S BEDROOM - DAY

Suddenly we hear footsteps approaching and the camera spins
around. To our shock and amazement we see BILL, BOB's
father, standing there. It takes us amoment to realize
that this is an image from many years before. BOBBIE is
sitting scrunched up on the floor. His father reaches in
and pulls him from the closet.

                    BILL
          Bobbie what are you doing in there?
          You get out of there right now.
          What the hell is going on, huh?
          What's this about a circus?

                    BOBBIE
          Nothing. I didn't do anything.

                    BILL
          You lying again?

                    BOBBIE
          You're the liar. You're the liar.
          You said you were going to take us
          to the circus. You promised. We
          were all dressed to go. Paul and
          me, we were all dressed. You
          promised.

                    BILL
          I did not promise. I said I'd try.
          I can't help it if I had to work.

                                              (CONTINUED)

76 CONTINUED:

> BOBBIE
> You always work. You promise things but you never do them.

> BILL
> What do you want? Do you want food on the table? People have to work.

> BOBBIE
> That's all you ever do. You're never ever home. You never do anything with us. I hate you. I hate you.

He jumps back into the closet and pulls the door shut.

77 INT. HOTEL ROOM - LATE AFTERNOON

CUT TO THE DOOR OF A HOTEL HONOR BAR as BOB pulls it open and reaches in for a club soda. Grabbing it, he returns quickly to the bed and hands it to GAIL. She is sitting propped up against the headboard. The mattress is covered with bags of Fritos and M&M's. BOB walks excitedly around the room. He pops open a Coke can.

> GAIL
> I've never heard that story. How come you never told me?

> BOB
> I totally forgot it until today. Isn't that incredible? I blanked it out. Can you imagine? I invited the entire class to a circus in my backyard. God. I can't believe I ever did something like that. Why would I do that?

> GAIL
> Maybe...for attention.

> BOB
> (considering her words)
> Yeah...maybe. I don't know.
> (pause)
> It's amazing, huh? I really thought it would be there when I got home from school. I really believed.

> GAIL
> (she sings)
> "...some day I'll wish upon a star and wake up where the clouds are far behind me."

(CONTINUED)

77 CONTINUED:

> BOB
> What is that?

> GAIL
> "Where troubles melt like lemon drops, away above the chimney tops, that's where you'll find me. Somewhere, over the rainbow..."

> BOB
> (holding up his hands)
> Okay, okay.

> GAIL
> (smiling)
> "blue birds fly..."
> (she stops)
> You were a believer.

> BOB
> Amazing... I don't even know who that person was.

> GAIL
> Oh come on. It sounds just like you.

> BOB
> What do you mean?

> GAIL
> You're still the ringmaster. Bob Jones, Public Relations. Except instead of wishing for circuses, you're creating them. You've got twenty rings...all going at the same time. It's so sweet. In some ways you're still that little boy...

GAIL reaches over and strokes his neck. BOB smiles.

78 INT. HOTEL ROOM - SHOWER - LATE AFTERNOON

GAIL gets out of the shower and dries off. She is singing to herself. She looks in the mirror and admires her full breasts and growing belly. She smiles sweetly.

79 EXT. HOTEL BALCONY - LATE AFTERNOON

BOB is standing on the tiny hotel balcony staring up at the evening sky. Suddenly he sees a star glimmering on the horizon. He almost seems embarrassed by it. Then, after a moment, an innocent, childlike look comes over his face. Suddenly, under his breath, he murmurs.

(CONTINUED)

79 CONTINUED: 79

>   BOB
>   Star light, star bright, first star
>   I see tonight, I wish I may, I wish
>   I might, have the wish I wish
>   tonight.
>   (silence)
>   Dear God, let me live long enough
>   to see my child. That's all I ask.

The camera holds on the sky.

80 EXT. FAMILY HOUSE - EVENING   80

We see a video of GAIL walking up to a traditional suburban house.

>   GAIL (V.O.)
>   How do I look?

The camera stops to look at her.

>   BOB (V.O.)
>   It's too dark to tell!

>   GAIL
>   I feel fat.

>   BOB (V.O.)
>   What do mean fat? You're pregnant.
>   Come on. These are peasants here.
>   You could weigh three hundred
>   pounds and you'd still look thin.
>   Besides, they love you.

At that instant the door opens. A heavyset woman looks out and screams.

>   SOPHIA
>   Bobbie! Bobbie! Oh my God, it's
>   Bobbie!

>   BOB
>   Aunt Sophia!

COUSIN NADIA screams out.

>   NADIA
>   Bobbie!

81   INT. FAMILY HOUSE - ENTRY WAY - EVENING   81

Suddenly we hear everyone inside yelling "Bobbie" too. The entry way fills with a crush of relatives, most of them overweight. BOB and GAIL are pulled into the house. The camera is still running. A maze of faces rush toward the camera. In the background we see a dining table piled high with food. People are swarming everywhere. BOB is overwhelmed.

                    HENRY
          Mr. Hollywood. How are things in
          movieland? You look great.

                    TEKLA
          Bobbie, Bobbie, gimme a kiss, come
          here.

                    SONIA
          Gail, let me look at you. Look at
          that tummy.

Overwhelmed by the melee, the camera is turned off.

82   OMIT   82

82A INT. KITCHEN - LATER   82A

The video camera studies the kitchen counter overflowing with food. Relatives are heaping piles of it onto their plates. BOB turns the camera on himself.

                    BOB
          Do you believe this? Have you ever
          seen so much food.

AUNT SONIA looks up at BOB and smiles.

                    SONIA
          What's the matter, your wife
          doesn't feed you? You're too thin.
          Have some piroghi. Eat.

She shoves a plate of food toward him. The screen goes black.

83   INT. HOUSE - LATER   83

Relatives are seated everywhere, on card table chairs, on the arms of couches, finishing dessert.

                                                       (CONTINUED)

83 CONTINUED:

From the dining room BOB can pan the entire house, the living room the kitchen and the family room beyond. Everyone seems happy. There is a warm feeling in the house.

Suddenly UNCLE HENRY sticks his head in front of the lens.

> HENRY
> Hey Bob, you ever gonna come out from behind that thing?

We see BOB contemplate the idea for a moment and then change his mind.

> BOB (V.O.)
> Nah

HENRY looks at him surprised. BOB smiles.

> BOB
> (continuing)
> Just kidding.

He pushes the off switch and the screen goes black.

84 INT. LIVING ROOM - NIGHT

Things are calmer now. Most of the relatives have left. Only the immediate family remains sitting quietly on sofas and chairs. The video camera is focused on PAUL.

> BOB (V.O.)
> Okay Paul, I'm ready.

PAUL looks very uncomfortable.

> PAUL
> Okay. Hi. I'm Paul. I'm your uncle. Your father's baby brother. The one he hasn't talked to in nearly two years. (I got that in there). And this is my fiancée, Anya, over here. Anya Stasiuk.

> ANYA (V.O.)
> Not for long.

The camera swerves to show a sweet and slightly plump young woman sitting adoringly beside him. She nods hello.

> PAUL (V.O.)
> And that's her parents over there, Lida and Nestor.

(CONTINUED)

84   CONTINUED:

The camera swerves again to show a couple in their early fifties waving at the lens.

The camera pans over to a grizzly old man sitting in an overstuffed chair smoking a cigarette. He is half asleep.

> BOB (V.O.)
> And that's my dad, Bill Ivanovich. Your grandfather. Dad, wake up. Blow away some of the smoke and say hello.

BILL'S eyes flash open, trying to pretend he is awake.

> BILL
> Hello.

> BOB (V.O.)
> Say it like you mean it.

> BILL
> Mean what?

> BOB (V.O.)
> For posterity. For your grandchild.

> BILL
> Hello.

> BOB (V.O.)
> A man of many words.

> ROSE (O.S.)
> Take that cigarette out of your mouth. You want your grandchild to see you like that? That thing's gonna kill you.

> BILL
> Don't start.

The camera moves to a large and not especially attractive woman sitting in a hardback chair. She is nearly unrecognizable from the woman we saw early in the film. She looks into the camera.

> ROSE
> He's coughing his life away.

> BILL (V.O.)
> Don't gimme that! Cigarettes don't kill you.

The camera swerves to BILL.

(CONTINUED)

84   CONTINUED: 2   84

                    ROSE (O.S.)
          That's not what the surgeon general
          says.

                    BILL
          What does he know?

And back to ROSE.

                    BOB (V.O.)
          And this is my mom, your
          grandmother...Rose. Say something
          Mom.

ROSE looks sternly into the camera.

                    ROSE
          I've got nothing to say. Stop
          hiding behind that thing.
                    (holding her hand up to
                     block the lens)
          Turn it off already. You got family
          here. Let us see you.

                    BOB
          Mom, it's not a line up - we're not
          the mafia here.

                    ROSE
          Turn it off.

Her hand covers the entire lens. The screen goes black.

85   INT. HOTEL ROOM - NIGHT   85

The door opens on BOB and GAIL'S hotel room as they enter
and begin to casually get out of their clothes.

                                                      (CONTINUED)

85 CONTINUED:

The camera follows them as they prepare for bed.

>   GAIL
>   Oh God, let me get out of this
>   thing.

She tosses her skirt over the corner chair. BOB throws his pants on top of hers.

>   BOB
>   It's so scary. The smartest thing
>   I ever did was to get away from
>   here.

>   GAIL
>   They really love you though.
>   Underneath it all, you can feel it.
>   You really can.

>   BOB
>   What are you feeling with, your big
>   toe? I don't feel a thing.
>   (he shakes his head)
>   Poor Paul. He had his chance to
>   escape. He blew it.

>   GAIL
>   It was his choice.

>   BOB
>   The choice of a coward.

>   GAIL
>   I don't know.

>   BOB
>   Believe me. And this Anya. She's
>   the back wall of a handball court.
>   I mean, look at her. She never met
>   a saturated fat she didn't like.

>   GAIL
>   I gather then you liked her.

>   BOB
>   If he'd only listened to me. There
>   were thousands of great jobs in
>   L.A. Great women. Look at him,
>   stuck in the junk business with my
>   father and in bed with that blob.
>   No wonder he takes the tow truck
>   home.

(CONTINUED)

85   CONTINUED: 2

> GAIL
> Come on. You're here to make peace. Enjoy them for what they are. Accept them. They're yours.
>
> BOB
> Whose side are you on?
>
> GAIL
> On the side of happiness. I think they're happy, Bob.
>   (pause)
> Are you so happy?
>
> BOB
>   (hesitating)
> I have extenuating circumstances.
>
> GAIL
> Who doesn't?
>
> BOB
>   (annoyed, turning away)
> Well, mine are just a little more extenuating than most.

He walks away. GAIL turns to him understandingly.

> GAIL
> I know.

Half undressed, BOB goes into the bathroom. GAIL follows after him. He begins to brush his teeth.

> GAIL
>   (continuing)
> So, are you going to say anything to anyone? They don't even know you're sick.
>
> BOB
> I don't want their sympathy.
>
> GAIL
> Is that fair to them?
>
> BOB
> It's fair to me. Look, I made the trip. I'm here. I'm behaving myself. So just leave me alone, okay?
>
> GAIL
> Anything you say.

(CONTINUED)

85 CONTINUED: 3

She turns and walks back into the bedroom. BOB stands there, angry and alone, still brushing his teeth. After a moment he stops, the toothbrush still in his mouth. There is a curious look on his face. He begins moving the toothbrush slowly, as if caressing each tooth. Suddenly he reaches up with his hand and touches his mouth, his lips, his tongue, his cheeks. There is a powerful longing in his eyes. It is a surprising existential moment, an unexpected whiff of mortality.

85A EXT. CHURCH - DAY

The camera pans down from Byzantine church spires and reveals PAUL and ANYA pulling up to their wedding in a horse drawn carriage. Six bridesmaids and six best men are waiting for them on the church steps.

86 INT. CHURCH - DAY

The church choir begins to sing. A quick pan of the wedding guests reveals a sea of video cameras recording the event. Add in the Kodak Instamatics and hardly anyone is viewing the proceedings through their normal eyes.

The wedding procession begins. A sea of attendants in taffeta dresses and tuxedos sweeps down the aisle. The bride's mother follows, looking radiant. ROSE and BILL seem awkward and out of their element.

ANYA walks down the aisle with her father and approaches the altar. She looks lovely. PAUL steps forward to greet her. GAIL, standing nearby, is crying. BOB, PAUL'S best man, looks over at her and winks.

CUT TO CROWNS being placed on the wedding couple's heads. A professional video crew documents every move.

CUT TO ICONS being blessed on the altar before them.

CUT TO the wedding couple walking around the altar.

CUT TO children asleep on a pew.

CUT TO an old married couple holding hands warmly.

CUT TO BILL and ROSE standing stoically, a hint of emotion buried deeply in their eyes.

CUT TO THE PRIEST placing a wedding ring on PAUL'S finger.

(CONTINUED)

86 CONTINUED:

CUT TO an unexpected video image of BOB. We can see in his face that he is holding back emotions. Suddenly a tear escapes down his cheeks. As he grabs a handkerchief to wipe it away he becomes aware that someone is filming him. He turns and glances into the lens.

CUT TO GAIL as she lowers the video camera and shrugs innocently. BOB shakes his head. She smiles apologetically and throws him a kiss.

CUT TO THE PRIEST pronouncing the couple man and wife. They kiss. The choir sings. PAUL takes ANYA and escorts her up the aisle. Attendants rush after them.

87 INT. CHURCH SOCIAL HALL - DAY

Deafening ethnic music fills the air. A Ukrainian M.C. stands on the stage of a large social hall in front of a large band. We watch him through BOB'S video.

> M.C.
> And now ladies and gentlemen, let us rise to welcome our bride and groom as they pass beneath the "courduvai" our traditional twisted bread symbolizing the happy and unhappy moments that are all part of one's life. A big hand for Paul and Anya.

There is a musical fanfare as PAUL and ANYA step under the bread and then carry it around the room. People applaud and bang their glasses in celebration. BOB turns his camera on GAIL. She raises her glass.

> GAIL
> To happiness

BOB nods.

BOB videos a mechanical bride and groom rotating next to an ice swan on the appetizer buffet. Behind it we see the head table. A lot of overweight people are eating. Suddenly a voluptuous blonde walks by. BOB zooms into to her as she walks to her table and then turns the camera on himself.

> BOB
> No way. She must be at the wrong wedding.

Loud polka music fills the air: "Roll out the Barrel". We see images of BILL dancing with ROSE and UNCLE HENRY dancing with GAIL. GAIL can't stop laughing. AUNT SONIA and AUNT TEKLA are dancing together.

(CONTINUED)

87 CONTINUED:

LIDA and NESTOR are trying to do the polka but don't know how. One couple is dancing with three children, one in a backpack, and two swirling around their feet. PAUL and ANYA are dancing slowly and romantically in the middle of the crowd. People eye them lovingly.

Rock and roll music explodes from the band. Bridesmaids in taffeta dresses toss off their shoes and jump onto the dance floor.

BOB aims his camera at different tables of people who aren't dancing. At one table all the relatives offer congratulations to the bride and groom in unison.

> RELATIVES
> Stoli! Stolat!

At another table the relatives seem to speak only Ukrainian. The eldest man at the table offers a toast in his native language. Everyone else at the table nods in agreement.

BOB circles a third table.

> UNCLE JIMMY
> I wish you everything. The best in all your life. Everything. The best...forever. Thank you.

An aunt waves him on, embarrassed. Another woman pipes in.

> AUNT ELENA
> Make lots of babies.

Everyone at the table agrees and cheers wholeheartedly.

CUT TO a table of black people, probably workers at the scrap yard. A large man speaks up.

> MAN
> Hey Paul and Anya, may all your ups and downs be between the sheets.

Everyone laughs and calls out "amen".

> WOMAN
> Do it tonight. Everything. Everything.

> GROUP
> Yeah!

Lively Ukrainian folk music erupts from the band. A circle of dancers forms in the middle of the dance floor. Instantly a group of women link arms and enter the middle.

(CONTINUED)

87 CONTINUED: 2

It is like a scene from "Seven Brides for Seven Brothers" or "Fiddler on the Roof". They dance in spectacular unison. After a few moments they retreat into the circle and a new group of women emerges. They are followed by two young men doing the kazatski. Everyone applauds.

PAUL motions for BOB to dance the kazatski with him. He refuses. Everyone encourages him to go ahead. Shamed into it, BOB enters the circle with his brother. The music sweeps them up instantly. It is amazing to watch them. It is as if twenty five years disappears and they are young men together. Knees bent, their feet fly into the air. GAIL watches her husband in wide-eyed disbelief. She has never seen this side of him. A smile breaks out on BOB'S face. PAUL grins at him. ROSE and BILL watch happily. ROSE takes BILL'S hand. The circle around them is full of joy.

CUT TO BOB sitting at a table sweating and catching his breath. GAIL is fanning him with her napkin. He is all smiles.

                    GAIL
      Want to dance some more?

                    BOB
          (shaking his head)
 Not me. I've got work to do.

88 OMIT

88A INT. CHURCH - DAY

A middle aged woman is seen in closeup looking into the camera. She is sitting in the choir loft of the church.

                  BOB (V.O.)
    Okay, tell us who you are.

                  NADIA
    Hi, my name is Nadia and I'm Bob's
    first cousin on his father's side.
    My father Nicholas is Bill's
    brother. You got that?

                  BOB (V.O.)
    Got it. So Nadia. You probably,
    more than anybody, remember me as a
    child. Why don't you just tell us
    a few things about me that might be
    interesting to my kid.

                                                   (CONTINUED)

88A CONTINUED:

                    NADIA
          A few things? I could talk for
          hours. You were a sex maniac. I
          mean that. If your kid has your
          genes, he's in big trouble. You
          always wanted to tie me up and take
          off all my clothes.

                    BOB (V.O.)
          Oh, come on!

                    NADIA
          It's true! You got my blouse off
          under your parents' bed, the four
          poster. You remember? We were
          hiding from the Germans. And that
          time in the shower at Grandma's
          house...

                    BOB (V.O.)
          How do you remember all this?

                    NADIA
          How could I forget?

88B INT. CHURCH - DAY

JUMP CUT TO COUSIN TANIA standing in the stairwell outside
the reception area.

                    TANIA
          ... and how about the time we used
          to play doctor together. You
          always wanted to give me a shot,
          right here.
                    (she points to her
                     butt)
          And you wouldn't do it through my
          panties either. I had to pull them
          down.

88C INT. CHURCH - DAY

JUMP TO COUSIN ALYISHA, sitting on a desk in a small church
classroom.

                    ALYISHA
                    (she laughs)
          ... and remember the time in
          Sophia's basement, you were all
          naked and we covered you up with
          toys. You were so kinky. Those
          were wonderful days, so innocent.

                                              (CONTINUED)

88C CONTINUED:

BOB, red-faced, puts the camera down.

> ALYISHA
> (continuing)
> Oh, I'm Sorry. I'm embarrassing you.

> BOB
> It's okay. Wasn't there anything else?

> ALYISHA
> Like what? What exactly are you looking for?

> BOB
> I wish I knew.

89 EXT. CHURCH GROUNDS - DAY

CUT TO AUNT TEKLA sitting on the steps in front of the church.

> TEKLA
> Hi. I'm Aunt Tekla and I remember you were the cutest little blonde-headed boy you've ever seen. You were so sweet. Still are. I could pinch you right now. Come here, gimme a big wet one, a blubber belly kiss.

> BOB (V.O.)
> Well, it's tempting Aunt Tekla. Just tell me a little bit more first.

> TEKLA
> More? Let's see.
> (she thinks a moment)
> You were funny, the funniest child. You would do whatever it took to make people laugh. Like the time you wrote "I love you Mom," with lipstick all over the living room couch. I laughed so hard...your mother didn't talk to me for a week. Or the time you filled your father's gas tank with water and he had to take the bus to Ypsilanti. He didn't laugh either, I'll tell you that. You were such a little devil.

(CONTINUED)

89   CONTINUED:

               BOB (V.O.)
          Why? Why was I like that?

TEKLA shrugs.

               TEKLA
          Who knows? Come on. Gimme that
          kiss. A big wet one.

She rushes the camera. The screen goes blank.

90   INT. CHURCH - DAY

CUT TO UNCLE HENRY and AUNT SONIA sitting on the steps in the social hall. We can see the dancing through the glass door behind them.

               HENRY
          You were a cool customer, distant
          like your father. A dreamer. You
          were both dreamers.

               BOB (V.O.)
          My father was a dreamer?

               HENRY
          Of course he was a dreamer. Where
          do you think you got it from? He
          always wanted to be a builder, to
          build houses, to build empires.
          Your mother took the dreams out of
          him.

               SONIA
          That's not true. His head was
          always in the clouds. Your
          mother's the one who made him work.
          Without your mother, you would've
          been a homeless person today. She
          gave you everything. She loved
          you.

BOB rolls his eyes.

               SONIA
               (continuing)
          She did. She loved you.

               BOB
          Yeah. She loved the garden too but
          at least the cabbage got a squeeze
          every now and then.

                                        (CONTINUED)

90 CONTINUED:

>   SONIA
>   Look, she was a simple woman. Her
>   life didn't revolve around
>   emotions. To her, washing the
>   clothes was an expression of love.

Suddenly ANDREA, another cousin, comes running from the social hall. The music blares as the glass door swings open.

>   ANDREA
>   Hurry, you should see this. Uncle
>   Alexi dancing with Aunt Sophia.
>   It's the most amazing thing, a
>   miracle. They haven't talked in
>   twenty years. God, I never thought
>   I'd live to see the day. Come on.

90A INT. CHURCH - DAY

BOB, ANDREA, SONIA, and HENRY hurry up the steps to observe the dancing. Sure enough AUNT SOPHIA is dancing with UNCLE ALEXI. Bob zooms into them.

>   ANDREA
>   It's so beautiful. That's what
>   life is all about, huh? To be
>   together. Not to fight. God, I'm
>   so happy I could cry.

Suddenly we hear a gasp as the camera wobbles and BOB leans against the door. ANDREA looks at him, concerned.

>   ANDREA (V.O.)
>   Bobbie, are you...?

>   BOB
>   I'm okay. Gail!? Where's Gail!

91 INT. CHURCH OFFICE - DAY

BOB is lying on an office couch with GAIL beside him. He looks pale and weak. GAIL lowers a glass of water to the desk top. ANDREA and several bystanders peek in the door.

>   ANDREA
>   Is he all right?

>   GAIL
>   He's fine. Nothing to worry about.
>   Just a little blood sugar. It's all
>   under control.

(CONTINUED)

91   CONTINUED:

                    ANDREA
          Scared me half to death.

                    GAIL
          Don't worry, really. Ten minutes
          he'll be as good as new.

ANDREA nods and closes the door. BOB tries to prop his head
up with his arms. He is already looking better. GAIL sits
down beside him.

                    BOB
          Thanks.
                    (they sit a moment in
                     silence)
          I think I was dizzy from holding the
          camera all day.

                    GAIL
          Or maybe the dancing.

                    BOB
          Maybe. It's so incredible. This
          videotape. It's like an
          archaeological dig...the ruins of
          me. I was a sexual pervert
          at the age of five. Can you believe
          that?

                    GAIL
                    (smiling)
          Yeah!

She leans over and gives him a big kiss. It is full of
love. He looks up at her, surprised.

                    BOB
          Hey, we're in church.

GAIL laughs.

                    BOB
                    (continuing)
          I used to think I knew all the
          answers. Now I don't even know the
          questions. What is that all about?

                    GAIL
          Sounds like progress to me.

She squeezes his hand.

                                            (CONTINUED)

91   CONTINUED: 2   91

92   INT. FAMILY HOUSE - LIVING ROOM - NIGHT   92

PAUL, ROSE, BILL, and GAIL are sitting close together on the "L" shaped sectional couch in the family room. BOB is on the floor near the fire place video taping the event. ANYA is walking in from the kitchen carrying a tray of coffee and left over wedding cake. She sets it down on the coffee table and then squeezes in beside her husband. The entire house seems filled with the remains of the wedding, floral centerpieces, balloons, presents.

                    ROSE
          Four tornados I said. Not twelve.
          The day you were born there were
          four tornados, one in Hamtramck,
          and three in Detroit. And nobody
          was killed. You exaggerate things.

                    BOB (V.O.)
          But you did say I was a born
          disaster. That's a quote, right?

                    ROSE
          When you were four, yes...a holy
          terror.

                    BOB (V.O.)
          How 'bout when I was ten?

                    ROSE
          You were different at ten. You
          used to disappear into the basement
          for hours. You'd play with your
          trains.

                    BILL
          We never saw you.

                    BOB (V.O.)
          Why? Why happened? Why did I
          disappear?

                    ROSE
          It's just the way you were.

                    BILL
          You were ashamed of us by then.
          You hid everything from us. You'd
          never bring your friends home. One
          day your mother went to school to
          see your teacher and you pretended
          not to know her, not to know your
          own mother. She cried for two
          days.

                                              (CONTINUED)

92 CONTINUED: 92

> PAUL
> Dad. Come on. Not again.
> (to ANYA)
> What did I tell you? Every time they get together...

BOB continues aiming the camera at his father, but he is no longer looking through it.

> BOB
> So what do you think? Why do you think I did that?

> ROSE
> It was a long time ago.

> BILL
> You always thought you were too good for us. That was your problem.
> (he leans into the camera)
> I want your kid should know that his father was too good for his own family, that the first chance he gets, he runs away, he changes his name, and doesn't even come back.

> BOB
> You're changing the subject.

> BILL
> I'm not changing anything. You're the one who changes things. Jones. What's the matter? You don't like my name, your father's name, your grandfather's name?

> BOB
> Dad, please.

BOB, exasperated, turns the camera off.

> BILL
> You change everything. You run from everything.

> BOB
> I never ran. I left. I wanted a life.

(CONTINUED)

BILL
You can't have a life with your family? If it wasn't for your wife, for her phone calls, you'd be a dead man to us, and that's the truth.

BOB
What do you want me to do? You want me to call and listen to this same stuff, over and over. How can I do that? How can a rational person do that?

BILL
A man who loves his family calls them.

GAIL
Dad...he really does love you.

BILL
Not in my book.

BOB
You talk about love. I've lived in Los Angeles ten years and not once have you attempted to visit, to see the business I've created, the life I've made.

PAUL
You know Mom doesn't fly.

BOB
She ever hear of trains?

ROSE
It's too far. I can't go that far.

BOB
Exactly.

ROSE
Maybe when the baby...

BOB
Yeah, sure... Look what does it matter? We'd just hack over this same shit anyway. God, this gets so boring. How do lives come to this?

BOB begins putting the camera back into the case. There is a long silence. No one speaks.

93   EXT. FAMILY HOUSE - NIGHT   93

BOB and PAUL are sitting quietly on a swing set in the large communal yard space behind their parent's home.

They are lit by the light from neighbors' windows.

>   PAUL
>   Hippopotamus !
>
>   BOB
>   What?
>
>   PAUL
>   You don't remember "hippopotamus"?
>
>   BOB
>   What are you talking about?
>
>   PAUL
>   It was your secret weapon. All you
>   had to do was say "hippopotamus"
>   and I would fall on the floor
>   laughing. It got me every time.
>
>   BOB
>   It sounds familiar.
>
>   PAUL
>   Whenever I think of it, I still
>   smile inside. It was a gift you
>   gave me. One of the few.
>
>   BOB
>   Have I been that terrible?
>
>   PAUL
>   Depends on how you define "that".
>
>   BOB
>   Thanks.

They turn a corner and head toward home. For a moment they walk in silence and then PAUL continues.

>   PAUL
>   I love you Bob, but, I gotta
>   tell you something, you can be a
>   stuck up, arrogant son of a bitch,
>   you know that? I mean, you stop
>   talking to me because I make a
>   career choice you don't approve
>   of. What kind of bullshit is
>   that?
>
>   BOB
>   That's not true. You rejected me.

(CONTINUED)

93   CONTINUED:

> PAUL
> No. I rejected Los Angeles. I couldn't live your life out there. I needed my friends. I needed family. All you cared about was business. In two weeks I saw you what, two times for dinner? And even then, I felt like a client. I watched what happened as you climbed the ladder. I didn't want to follow. I didn't want to become that kind of person.
>
> BOB
> I could have gotten you a great job, starting at $60,000. How could you pass that up to work in a junk yard?
>
> PAUL
> Scrap metal. Scrap metal.
>
> BOB
> It's junk. It's always been junk.
>
> PAUL
> That's where we differ. You hated Dad for being a junk man. I've loved him for being a hard worker. That's the difference.
>
> BOB
> I never said I hated him.
>
> PAUL
> Oh yes you have. But let's forget the semantics, okay? Look, he's your dad, for God's sake. You used to bounce up and down on his knee. He took you on the train to Cleveland. You used to talk about that all the time when we were kids, how he took you in the Pullman car, just the two of you. I remember the look in your eye. What happened to that look?
>
> BOB
> I don't know.

They sit down on the porch stoop just outside the door.

(CONTINUED)

93   CONTINUED: 2   93

                        PAUL
            It's so funny, Bob. For all your
            complaining about Dad, I get the
            sense you're gonna turn out just
            like him.

BOB is stung by the comment. It goes deep inside him. They
sit for a moment in silence.

                        PAUL
                    (continuing)
            I know you have no respect for us,
            for the whole family, but we're
            actually a pretty good bunch. We
            love each other, we care for each
            other. You're sitting in Los
            Angeles, a million miles away.
            Who's caring for you Bob? I met
            your friends. Thank God you've got
            Gail. That's all I can say. Look,
            I gotta go in. I really do. I'm
            leaving for my honeymoon in half an
            hour.
                    (he stands up)
            I just hope, when your kid is born,
            it'll love you more than you love
            us. That's all I hope.

BOB puts his hand lovingly on his brother's shoulder. PAUL
reaches out and hugs him. For a moment BOB is tentative as
he hugs him back but then as PAUL is about to pull away BOB
holds on. It is a deeply felt, loving embrace. After a
moment they separate.

                        PAUL
                    (continuing)
            Show it to them too. They're the
            ones that need to see it.

                        BOB
            Maybe, one day.

BOB sits back down on the swing.

                        PAUL
            Bob, you're a grown man for God's
            sake. How long can you carry this
            with you? They are not going to be
            around forever you know.

He kisses his brother on the top of the head and then turns
and enters the house. For a long time BOB just sits there,
lost in thought. He does not move.

94   EXT. AVIS RENTALS, DETROIT AIRPORT - DAY   94

BOB and GAIL are running for the Avis bus to take them to
the terminal. It has stopped to wait for them.

                                                    (CONTINUED)

94   CONTINUED: 94

BOB is huffing and puffing. Suddenly he puts the luggage down. The effort is too much for him. There is a frightened look on his face.

>   GAIL
>   What's the matter?

>   BOB
>   I can't make it. I don't know...I
>   just can't...

GAIL looks concerned. She hurries back and grabs his luggage. He stands there helplessly, unable to assist.

>   BOB
>   I blew it.

>   GAIL
>   (looking at him oddly)
>   Bob, come on. The bus.

>   BOB
>   (not moving)
>   I didn't resolve...anything.

>   GAIL
>   Bob, it's about to leave.

GAIL grabs the bags and struggles toward the bus. We sense a feeling of weakness and shame in BOB'S eyes. The driver of the bus steps down and gives them a hand.

95   INT. BUS - DAY   95

BOB and GAIL are sitting at the back of the bus. They are the only passengers. Neither of them are talking. Suddenly GAIL looks up at BOB. He seems very sad.

>   GAIL
>   Are you alright?

>   BOB
>   This was my last trip home.

GAIL is about to contradict him but then holds herself back. The camera focuses on him as he contemplates what he has said. His face is awash in emotion that he will not let out. GAIL moves her foot close to his. He closes his eyes.

96   INT. MR. HO'S OFFICE - DAY - RAIN   96

BOB is lying on the healer's table as MR. HO moves his hands over BOB's chest. We can almost see rays of energy radiating from his palms. We can hear rain outside the window.

> BOB
> It's not getting any better.

> MR. HO
> You don't have to tell me. I can see. It's still there...right there. The anger, the fear.
> (he holds his hands
> over BOB'S sternum)
> You are not a very good student. Life is trying to teach you and you don't listen. Opportunities come and you don't see them.

> BOB
> How can you say that? I listened. I did exactly what you said. I flew to Detroit, two thousand miles, just to see my parents.

> MR. HO
> I didn't tell you to see your parents. I just said you needed to forgive. There's only one place you need to go.

> BOB
> Where?

> MR. HO
> Your heart.

> BOB
> My heart! Great! And how exactly does one get there?

He takes BOB'S hand and places it over his chest.

> MR. HO
> (his voice lowering)
> With your mind. Feel into the center of your chest. Imagine your finger pushing into it, deeper and deeper. When you start to feel happy, when you feel a sense of "well being," you are there. It is the place of love and forgiveness.

BOB stares at him oddly. MR. HO grows increasingly serious.

(CONTINUED)

96 CONTINUED:

>   MR. HO
>   (continuing)
>   Go there...soon.

97 INT. JONES BEDROOM - NIGHT

GAIL is lying in bed with a cassette recorder placed over
her ever-growing tummy. It is playing SOUTH PACIFIC
directly into the womb. BOB is lying beside her, his hands
over his chest. It is obvious that he is practicing what
MR. HO has taught him. There is a certain absurdity in what
they are doing. They both look at each other and laugh.

>   GAIL
>   I'm seeing Dr. Mills at 3:00
>   tomorrow. He's going to do the
>   ultrasound. If I find out the sex
>   of the baby, do you want me to tell
>   you?
>
>   BOB
>   (distracted)
>   Sure, that'd be great.

GAIL, anticipating his response, quietly looks away.

98 INT. OBSTETRICAL EXAMINING ROOM - DAY

GAIL is lying on an obstetrical examination table waiting
for the doctor when a nurse enters the room. GAIL looks up
and is shocked to see BOB following sheepishly behind her.
A huge grin appears on her face. Her eyes get all watery.

>   NURSE
>   Does he belong to you? I found him
>   wandering in the hall.
>
>   GAIL
>   Bob? What are you doing...?
>
>   BOB
>   I was in the neighborhood.

GAIL laughs and cries at the same time.

>   GAIL
>   Oh God. I don't believe this. I
>   really don't. You made my day.

BOB walks tentatively into the room. It is like alien
terrain to him. He seems especially uncomfortable.

(CONTINUED)

98   CONTINUED:

> NURSE
> The doctor will be right here. You wanna sit down?

> BOB
> Doesn't matter. Whatever. I don't care.

He doesn't sit. Instead he wanders around, gazing curiously at the machinery lining the walls. After a moment he walks over and unexpectedly puts his hand on GAIL'S stomach. She is deeply moved by this and can barely contain her emotion.

> GAIL
> What's happening to you? Are you changing in your old age?

BOB smiles softly. DR. MILLS enters the room and shakes hands with him.

> DR. MILLS
> Mr. Jones, I presume? It's a pleasure to meet you. I'm Dr. Mills.

> BOB
> How do you do?

He walks over to the sink, washes his hands, and puts on rubber gloves. After a moment he turns to BOB and GAIL. We sense a hesitation in his voice.

> DR. MILLS
> I just want to tell you that I think you're both very brave and remarkable people. That's all I want to say. I know this can't be easy for either of you.

BOB looks at GAIL, realizing that she's told him about his condition. She looks contrite. Unexpectedly there is a look of relief on his face.

He nods his head and squeezes GAIL'S hand. ANGLE ON THE NURSE in the corner of the room as she reaches for a Kleenex. THE DOCTOR places a small box over GAIL'S stomach.

> DR. MILLS
> This is a fetal doppler. It amplifies the sound of your baby's heart beat.

He moves it around her tummy. We hear strange static noises like a deep space probe, and then suddenly a regular beating rhythm is heard.

(CONTINUED)

98 CONTINUED: 2

>   DR. MILLS
>   (continuing)
>   That's it. That's the heart.

BOB smiles.

>   DR. MILLS
>   (continuing)
>   Okay. Let's take a look at the
>   baby with the ultrasound machine.
>   (pause)
>   This is going to be a little cold.
>   (he rubs some gel onto
>   Gail's stomach)

>   GAIL
>   A little cold!

>   DR. MILLS
>   Would you like me to videotape
>   this for you?

>   BOB
>   Can you? That'd be great.
>   (beat)
>   Amazing, huh? Home movies **before**
>   you're born.

THE DOCTOR turns on the ultrasound machine and presses the video button. A fuzzy image appears almost instantly. Unfortunately it is impossible to make out what it is. THE DOCTOR moves the small imaging device over GAIL'S stomach. For a while there are only obscure shadows. Then, suddenly, as if from out of the cosmic void, a tiny face appears, staring right at us. It is a moment of unexpected, power. BOB gasps and reaches for GAIL'S hand.

>   DR. MILLS
>   Well, what do you think? What a
>   beautiful profile. That's a
>   gorgeous baby.

Cut to BOB and GAIL, nearly breathless, watching the monitor. The camera holds on their faces and observes the powerful play of emotions moving across them. It is obvious that BOB is deeply affected by what he sees.

Suddenly the baby turns and THE DOCTOR repositions the device to observe other features. There is a track bar on the bottom of the screen and THE DOCTOR lines it up over what appears to be a hand. We watch him take a measurement. A computer readout interprets it.

>   DR. MILLS
>   This is good. You're in your
>   twenty-fourth week, your baby's
>   right on schedule.

(CONTINUED)

98   CONTINUED: 3   98

He moves the device again. Something indecipherable appears in front of them. THE DOCTOR is excited.

>   DR. MILLS
>   (continuing)
>   My, oh my, look at that. Would
>   you like to know the sex?

>   BOB AND GAIL
>   (unanimously)
>   Yes!

He points to an obscure nodule on the screen.

>   DR. MILLS
>   You have a son, a beautiful,
>   healthy looking son.

>   BOB
>   (amazed)
>   How can you tell?

>   DR. MILLS
>   (pointing to the
>   screen)
>   Either that or he's got three legs.

>   BOB
>   (thrilled)
>   A son!

GAIL, beaming, grabs his hand and suddenly all BOB'S defenses break down. With great effort he chokes back every ounce of emotion rising inside him. GAIL strokes his hand and starts to cry. DR. MILLS puts his arm around BOB'S shoulder.

This is more than the NURSE can bear. Grabbing a handful of tissues she hurries from the room.

99   OMIT   99

99A INT. WAITING ROOM - DAY   99A

THE NURSE hurries into the waiting room as SEVERAL PREGNANT LADIES look up. Nearly crying and smiling at the same time, she announces:

>   NURSE
>   It's a boy!

The ladies look at her curiously and nod their heads.

100   INT. RESTAURANT - NIGHT

BOB and GAIL are sitting next to one another at a snug but cozy table. A WAITER is pouring from a bottle of Perrier. As he steps out of frame we see that they are in a fancy restaurant.

BOB
God. I can't believe it. What are we going to call him? Have you even thought...?

GAIL
Mom wants me to name him after her father.

BOB
Zachary? Are you crazy?

GAIL
Zack.

BOB
No way. No son of mine. You don't know what it's like in school. They eat Zacks for breakfast.

GAIL
What else starts with Z? Zeus? Zirconia?

BOB
Forget Z.

GAIL
But my mother...

BOB
Forget your mother... This is our child. It'll be our name.
(thinking)
Robert Junior.

GAIL
Junior? I hate anything junior. It's so antiquated, so impersonal. He has to be his own person. He needs something to counteract Jones.

BOB
What's wrong with Jones?

(CONTINUED)

100   CONTINUED:

>   GAIL
>   I love Jones. But so did half of
>   the people in the last census. He
>   needs something distinctive.
>
>   BOB
>   You're right.
>
>   GAIL
>   Aloysius.
>   (she smiles)
>
>   BOB
>   It's distinctive.

The WAITER reappears, blocking the view.

>   WAITER
>   Have you decided?
>
>   BOB
>   Long way to go.
>
>   WAITER-
>   Okay. I'll be back in a few
>   minutes.
>
>   BOB
>   This could take a few days.

THE WAITER gives them a strange look. They smile.

101   INT. CAR - NIGHT

BOB and GAIL are driving home.

>   GAIL
>   Prometheus.
>
>   BOB
>   It has a ring to it. Agamemnon?
>
>   GAIL
>   Cute. Odysseus?
>
>   BOB
>   (shaking his head)
>   Forget the Greeks. Try something
>   Roman.
>
>   GAIL
>   Julius.

(CONTINUED)

101 CONTINUED:

> BOB
> Augustus.

> GAIL
> Caligula.

> BOB
> Stuart.

> GAIL
> (laughing)
> Stuart? That isn't Roman.

> BOB
> It's not?

They both laugh. Suddenly GAIL stops.

> GAIL
> Oh God, quick, feel. He's kicking.

She places BOB'S hand on her stomach.

> BOB
> Jesus, I feel that. I can feel his foot.

> GAIL
> You know what that means?

> BOB
> What?

> GAIL
> He hates "Stuart".

They laugh.

102 INT. JONES BEDROOM - NIGHT

BOB and GAIL stumble into their room, still laughing.

> BOB
> Josephat.

> GAIL
> Something thinner.

> BOB
> Anorexis.

> GAIL
> That's a girl's name.

(CONTINUED)

102 CONTINUED:

                    BOB
          Morton.

                    GAIL
          Morton?

                    BOB
          I don't know. It just came. A
          spontaneous emission.

                    GAIL
          Hold that thought.

She pushes him onto the bed and falls on top of him. They
begin to kiss. She reaches to unbuckle his belt.

                    BOB
          What are you doing? You sure you
          want to do this?

                    GAIL
          I'm sure.

                    BOB
          You're an amazing woman, you know
          that?

                    GAIL
          I must be. I live with you.

                    BOB
          Gee thanks. Am I really that
          difficult?

                    GAIL
          Some things you don't want to know.
                    (she smiles and grabs
                     him by the hair)
          Come here, you son-of-a-bitch.

He smiles as they kiss passionately and fall excitedly into
bed.

103 INT. TOYS R US - DAY

BOB is bumping his way down a crowded aisle and piling toy
upon toy into an overflowing cart. It is interesting to
watch him as he veers from infants' playthings to footballs
and chemistry sets. The piece de resistance is a seven foot
giraffe that wreaks havoc with the other customers and
standing displays.

104   INT. BOB'S OFFICE CONFERENCE ROOM - DAY   104

BOB and GAIL are surrounded by office personnel. BOB is showing off gifts from an office shower, children's clothes he is sure are too small for any human being to wear. He keeps measuring the outfits against his chest in amazement. He seems to have a preference for baseball outfits and football jerseys. Everyone ooohs and aaahhs.

105   INT. B. DALTON'S - DAY   105

BOB sits on the floor of a large bookstore, surrounded by piles of children's books. He is reading Dr. Seuss' "Green Eggs and Ham", and seems to be enjoying it immensely. A little boy stands over his shoulder. BOB smiles.

                    BOB
          This used to be my favorite book.

                    BOY
          Mine too.

CUT TO BOB reading.

                    BOB
          "Do you like green eggs and ham?"

The boy shakes his head "no". Bob smiles.

                    BOB
                 (continuing)
          "I do not like them Sam-I-am. I do
          not like green eggs and ham. Would
          you like them here or there? I
          would not like them here or there.
          I would not like them anywhere. I
          do not like green eggs and ham. I
          do not like them, Sam-I-am. Would
          you like them in a house? Would
          you like them with a mouse? I do
          not like them in a house. I do not
          like them with a mouse. I do not
          like them here or there. I do not
          like them anywhere. I do not like
          green eggs and ham. I do not like
          them Sam-I-am."

The camera pulls back to reveal several children sitting beside BOB, listening to him read. Grateful parents look down warmly.

106   INT. CHILDBIRTH CLASS - NIGHT   106

VIDEO IMAGE. A Fetus floats blissfully in the womb. We are watching the climactic moments of a documentary on fetal development. The imagery is stunning, even awesome, as it concludes its portrait of the beginnings of life.

>   NARRATOR
> And so the greatest journey of all, the journey of life, begins as a race between hundreds of millions of sperm, the very strongest challenging each other for the honor of bringing life to a remarkable new being - your baby. Even before birth we have proven ourselves. We are already winners. It is the miracle of life. In nine months your babies will experience an explosion of growth of unimaginable proportions. An entire body grows inside the protection of the womb, preparing us for an even greater journey beyond. Birth is the doorway to that journey, a voyage into the wonder and mystery of being. We are all on that voyage together.

The tape ends and we find ourselves in BOB and GAIL'S childbirth class. About eight couples are gathered around a television, staring wide-eyed at the tube as the documentary ends. After a moments silence BOB can be heard exclaiming.

>   BOB
> Yeah!

Everyone laughs.

CUT TO THE EIGHT WOMEN lying on the floor with their knees to their chests. In a long lens shot their tummies look like mountain ranges fading off into the distance. Eight husbands kneel in front of their wives, holding up their feet. The women are trying to breathe in short rapid breaths through pursed lips. GAIL is very pregnant.

>   INSTRUCTOR
> Don't hyperventilate. The idea is to stay focused on your breathing so you can remain relaxed, detached from the discomfort of the contractions. Okay now, on your sides. We'll work on the lower back.

(CONTINUED)

106 CONTINUED:

CUT TO THE WOMEN lying on their sides as their husbands massage their backs.

> INSTRUCTOR
> Okay daddies, good. Keep it gentle but firm. Very good.

107 INT. JONES BEDROOM - NIGHT

The image is suddenly reversed as we see BOB, in great pain, lying on his side, breathing rapidly through pursed lips. GAIL is massaging his back. We can tell from his grimace that this is not a practice session.

> GAIL
> Is it working?

> BOB
> No.

> GAIL
> Just what I needed to hear. Want me to stop?

> BOB
> No.

GAIL shrugs and keeps massaging. BOB keeps breathing. After a moment he slows down and rolls over. GAIL pulls back.

> GAIL
> What a team.
> (she leans into her
> pillow)
> So tell me, is this breathing all a load of crap?

> BOB
> (he shrugs)
> It's better than screaming.

> GAIL
> Great.

108 EXT. MAGIC MOUNTAIN - COLOSSUS FOOTPATH BRIDGE - DAY

BOB and GAIL are approaching the Serpent, the biggest roller coaster at Magic Mountain.

> GAIL
> Are you sure about this?

(CONTINUED)

108 CONTINUED: 108

> BOB
> It's been over thirty years. It's time I tried again.

> GAIL
> Maybe you should start on the Tilt-A-Whirl.

> BOB
> No way. I'm going straight for the core fear, right to the heart of darkness.

> GAIL
> I wish I could go with you.

> BOB
> Some things you need to do alone.

He heads off to get in line.

109 EXT. COLOSSUS LOADING PLATFORM - DAY 109

The coaster car pulls into the loading dock. BOB steps heroically inside. A TEN YEAR OLD BOY is ushered in beside him. The bar is lowered tightly to BOB'S lap. His face goes white. GAIL waves.

The coaster takes off, climbing the most enormous hill BOB has ever seen. His hands clutch the bar in panic.

110 EXT. COLOSSUS - DAY 110

> BOY
> You ever been on a coaster before?

> BOB
> Not since I was six. I was too afraid.

> BOY
> (wide-eyed)
> You're kidding? And now you picked the Serpent?

BOB freezes. His knuckles are turning white.

> BOY
> (continuing)
> If you really want to do it right, let go.

He raises his hands up into the air.

(CONTINUED)

110   CONTINUED:

                    BOB
          Are you crazy?

                    BOY
          You won't fall out. Trust me.

                    BOB
                (gripping tight)
          This is what I trust.
                (they reach the top)
          Oh God!

111   EXT. COLOSSUS - DAY

In two seconds they are speeding downward at 70 miles an hour. THE BOY keeps his hands up in the air and smiles joyfully. BOB, his face contorted in a state of total panic, closes his eyes. It is hard to tell what he is mumbling so furiously, but he appears to be praying. THE BOY looks over at him and smiles.

                    BOY
          Great, huh?

                    BOB
          How much longer?

                    BOY
          Just two more drops - but really
          great ones.

BOB gasps.

112   EXT. COLOSSUS LOADING PLATFORM - DAY

The coaster pulls into the station and an attendant pulls open the safety bar. BOB can barely loosen his fingers, so tightly are they holding on.

                    BOY
          You can let go now.

                    BOB
          I'm trying.

113   EXT. MAGIC MOUNTAIN - COLOSSUS FOOTPATH BRIDGE - DAY

GAIL'S smiling face as BOB wobbles toward her. He tries to appear triumphant as she goes to meet him.

                    GAIL
          My hero.

                                              (CONTINUED)

113   CONTINUED: 113

Just as she is about to embrace him he bends over and throws up all over the nearest bush. GAIL looks away. When he finally stands up he turns to her and smiles.

> BOB
> Still your hero?

> GAIL
> (grinning)
> You bet.

114   EXT. MAGIC MOUNTAIN - COLOSSUS PLAZA - DAY   114

CUT TO BOB AND GAIL leaving the roller coaster area. GAIL has to hold him up as his knees are still a bit unsteady.

> BOB
> You know what today is?

> GAIL
> No. What?

> BOB
> D-Day.

> GAIL
> D-Day?

> BOB
> Death day. I was supposed to be dead by today.

GAIL stops and looks at him. She touches his face.

> GAIL
> Oh Bob.

> BOB
> This is borrowed time.

There is a deep silent moment between them and then, slowly lovingly, they embrace. Music is playing over the park speakers. Unexpectedly BOB starts dancing with his wife, right in the middle of the walkway. People look at them oddly. GAIL is both amazed and a bit embarrassed, but BOB is oblivious to everyone. He just looks so happy. He doesn't seem to care.

115   INT. MR. HO'S OFFICE - NIGHT   115

BOB enters Mr. Ho's office, shakes his hand. There is a growing friendliness between them.

(CONTINUED)

115 CONTINUED:

Bob lies down on the table on his back. Mr. Ho has him turn onto his stomach.

                    BOB
          How'm I doin?

                    MR. HO
          You're still alive, aren't you?

                    BOB
               (smiling)
          I know. Remarkable, huh?

MR. HO appears to be pulling unseen acupuncture needles out of the air and placing them in the appropriate energy meridians of BOB'S body. BOB looks at him oddly but acceptingly and continues talking.

                    BOB
               (continuing)
          I saw my physician. He said the
          tumors appear to be shrinking. He
          was amazed. I was amazed. You
          know, it's funny. It's almost as
          if I can feel them shrinking.

                    MR. HO
          Why is that funny?

                    BOB
          Well, I don't mean funny funny.
          Just odd funny. I'm not used to
          feeling things like that.

                    MR. HO
          Then it's a good sign.

                    BOB
          All I can imagine is that you must
          be having some effect.

                    MR. HO
          Not me. It is the light that
          heals.

MR. HO uses his hands like a vacuum cleaner, sucking poisons out of BOB'S body, and then shaking the psychic debris into the air.

                    BOB
               (shaking his head)
          I don't get it. I don't have the
          slightest idea what's going on
          here. Who are you? What is it you
          do?

                                        (CONTINUED)

115 CONTINUED: 2   115

                    MR. HO
I'm a garbage man. I take out the garbage.

                    BOB
                 (grinning)
I knew you'd say something like that. You know, you never cease to amaze me.

MR. HO looks at BOB with a serious expression on his face.

                    MR. HO
Amazement is a waste of time. Quiet. Let me work.

116 INT. JONES BATHROOM - NIGHT   116

BOB is in the shower when GAIL enters the bathroom and knocks on the sliding door.

                    BOB
Yo.

                    GAIL
It's time.

                    BOB
For what?

                    GAIL
I'm having contractions. They're pretty close together.

                    BOB
Wait a minute. I can't hear you. What did you say?

                    GAIL
My contractions have started.

                    BOB
                (digging soap from his
                 ear)
Your contraption has what?

                    GAIL
We're having a baby.

                    BOB
Now? Now! Oh my God! Oh my God!

                               (CONTINUED)

116 CONTINUED:

He jumps from the shower, forgetting to dry himself and nearly kills himself on the wet floor.

> GAIL
> Dry off. You have time.

> BOB
> Dry off? Oh, Jesus, I'm soaking wet.

She throws him a towel.

> GAIL
> I'll be waiting. I'm nearly packed.

> BOB
> Stay calm.

> GAIL
> Who? Me?

117   OMIT

117A OMIT

117B OMIT

117C OMIT

118   INT. LABOR ROOM - NIGHT

A VIDEO IMAGE OF GAIL IN LABOR. She is trying to breathe but the pain is beyond her.

> GAIL
> (panting)
> Oh God! Oh God! Help me!
> (to BOB)
> Turn that fucking thing off!

The image goes dead.

CUT TO BOB rubbing an ice cube along GAIL'S mouth. Her tongue seeks out its moisture.

> GAIL
> (continuing)
> Oh honey, thank you. Stay with me. I love you. Oh God, it's coming!

She starts to pant. Her whole face contorts as the
contraction builds. BOB glances at his watch and times its
progression.

                    BOB
                 (shouting)
        Thirty seconds. Relax. Go with
        the flow. Just breathe. Let it
        happen. Relax. Relax. Breathe.
        Forty-five seconds. You're doing
        great.

                    GAIL
        Shut up!

BOB grows quiet. He looks hurt but understanding. GAIL
pants as though her life depended on it.

DR. MILLS walks in and turns to BOB.

                    DR. MILLS
        How's everyone doin'?

                                      (CONTINUED)

118   CONTINUED: 2   118

>   BOB
>   I don't know.
>
>   DR. MILLS
>   (to GAIL)
>   Let me check and see if we are
>   making any progress.

He does a quick examination and shakes his head.

>   BOB
>   Any better?
>
>   DR. MILLS
>   A little bit.
>   (to GAIL)
>   Your contractions are getting
>   further apart and need to be
>   closer together and more regular
>   if we are to make progress. I'm
>   going to start pitocin in order to
>   increase the strength and
>   frequency of your contractions.
>
>   GAIL
>   Increase? What do you mean
>   increase? Are you crazy?
>
>   DR. MILLS
>   It'll speed things along.

He turns and heads out into the hall. BOB goes after him.

119   INT. HOSPITAL HALLWAY - NIGHT   119

>   BOB
>   Is everything okay?
>
>   DR. MILLS
>   Everything is going well.

120   INT. LABOR ROOM - NIGHT   120

A HORRIBLE SCREAM. GAIL'S contractions quadruple in
intensity. BOB, standing beside her, looks like a basket
case. In truth there is nothing he can do. As it quiets
back down he leans close to her and gently strokes her
forehead.

>   BOB
>   I love you. I love you so much.
>
>   GAIL
>   Why did God do this?

(CONTINUED)

120 CONTINUED:

>   BOB
> To make life.

>   GAIL
> It's amazing there's a human race.

BOB smiles.

121 INT. DELIVERY ROOM - NIGHT

CUT TO THE LABOR ROOM BEING CONVERTED INTO THE DELIVERY ROOM as the labor bed is pulled in half and stirrups are added to the end. A new contraction starts almost immediately.

>   DR. MILLS
> Alright. Let's push again.

>   GAIL
> Oh God!

>   DR. MILLS
> Good. Very good. Everything's
> going great. Grab your camera.

>   BOB
> What?

>   DR. MILLS
> Here comes the head. Hurry up.
> How often do you get to see your
> baby being born?

BOB gabs his camera and holds it to his eye. Then, suddenly he lets it down.

>   DR. MILLS
> Aren't you going to shoot?

>   BOB
> Not yet. I want to see it with my
> own eyes.

An expression of total awe emerges on BOB'S face as GAIL struggles to push her son into the world.

>   DR. MILLS
> I got the head.

GAIL screams. BOB beams as he crosses over to GAIL'S side.

>   DR. MILLS
>   (continuing)
> One more push. Just one more.

(CONTINUED)

121   CONTINUED: 121

GAIL bears down. THE DOCTOR blocks our view for a moment and then pulls back. In that instant a new being emerges into the world. DR. MILLS holds him up smiling gleefully. BOB'S face is glowing. He reaches down and grabs hold of his wife. There is a sense of tremendous joy between them.

>   DR. MILLS
>   (continuing)
>   Here's your handsome son.

He places the baby on GAIL'S abdomen and the NURSE puts warm blankets around the baby.

>   GAIL
>   Get your camera.

BOB grabs the camera and zooms into a beautiful wiggling child, his limbs extended, clutching for life, reaching in all directions. A suction ball is inserted into his mouth and extracts excess liquids. Almost instantly we hear a loud gasp and then a tremendous cry. Even the nurses smile. BOB turns the camera to GAIL. The look on her face is full of wonder. BOB leans toward her and hits her in the head with the camera.

>   GAIL
>   Ouch.

The camera keeps running as BOB and GAIL hug. All we see is feet moving across the floor.

>   BOB (V.O.)
>   He's so beautiful.

BOB backs away and aims the camera at his wife and child. The smile on GAIL'S face is transcendent. It is the image of the Madonna and Child, of all mothers and all children in their first embrace.

>   DR. MILLS
>   Let me.

DR. MILLS reaches for the camera. Bob hands it to him and approaches his new family. The three of them entwine, hugging and smiling. It is a moment of consummate joy. DR. MILLS records the entire scene. He seems very happy.

(CONTINUED)

121   CONTINUED: 2   121

                              DR. MILLS
                    You did great.

BOB and GAIL beam back at him with enormous gratitude.

CUT TO A CLOSE UP OF BOB. For a second we catch him looking up toward the ceiling. His eyes flood with tears as his lips silently form two words.

                              BOB
                    Thank you.

MONTAGE

122   INT. INSERT - VIDEO - BIRTH ANNOUNCEMENT   122

We see a video image of the printed baby announcement welcoming Brian Zachary Jones into the world. It is accompanied by a recording of the trumpet opening from Masterpiece Theatre.

123   INT. JONES LIVING ROOM - DAY   123

The music continues over video closeups of the baby lying naked on a blanket in the middle of the living room floor. We see him from every conceivable angle. The camera lingers on his face, his hands, his buttocks. Every part of his tiny anatomy is worthy of adoration.

124   INT. JONES BEDROOM - DAY   124

NEW IMAGES of the baby nursing, rocking, burping and throwing up. We see pictures of him and GAIL, cooing, nuzzling, and falling asleep together.

125   INT. JONES BABY ROOM - DAY   125

IMAGES of the baby discovering his hands and playing with his feet. We observe as BOB changes the baby's diaper and tries to instruct GAIL in the use of the video camera.

                              BOB
                    No, don't use the zoom. Get over
                    to the side. Don't jiggle it so
                    much. Hold it steady.

Suddenly the baby pees all over BOB. GAIL laughs.

CUT TO IMAGES of the baby wearing sun glasses, Groucho glasses, BOB'S baseball caps.

126 EXT. JONES BACKYARD - DAY

IMAGES of GAIL and the baby on a swing approaching and receding from the camera.

The baby is wide-eyed with delight. The image switches to BOB coming down a slide, holding BRIAN in his lap. It is hard to tell who looks happier.

126A INT. JONES HOUSE - DAY

CUT TO IMAGES of the baby that fade in and out like still photos but are actually found video moments. We see the baby lying in a bouncer staring at the window. Fade to a shot of the baby lying on the bed next to a spray of fresh daisies. Fade into a shot of the baby's foot pressed up against BOB'S. Fade into an image of BRIAN smiling.

127 INT. JONES LIVING ROOM - DAY

IMAGES OF BOB naked, crawling and playing on the carpet with his infant son. He looks up surprised and embarrassed to see the camera rolling. We can hear GAIL laugh. Smiling, he picks up the baby. Holding him discretely, like a living fig leaf, he runs laughing toward the camera and blocks out the screen.

128 INT. R.A.JONES, PUBLIC RELATIONS - DAY

BOB parades the baby around for everyone to see. There is mass excitement. He is very proud. We see the baby sitting on BOB'S lap in BOB'S desk chair playing with a pen. Walter shoves a piece of paper in front of him.

                  WALTER
    Here, let him sign my raise.

129 EXT. JONES DRIVEWAY - DAY

BOB is standing between his BMW and his wife's Honda. He is delivering an "INSTRUCTIONAL VIDEO" to camera.

                  BOB
    The important thing about jumping a
    battery is the placement of the
    cable. Make sure you start with the
    red end of the cable attached to the
    positive pole on the dead car's
    battery.
                  (MORE)

(CONTINUED)

129 CONTINUED:
129

> BOB (CONT'D)
> Now if the batteries are old and you can't tell which is the positive and which is the negative...call a cab.

130 OMIT
130

130A INT. JONES KITCHEN - DAY
130A

BOB is feeding BRIAN solid food. Unfortunately very little goes into the baby's mouth. Most of it covers his cheeks and neck.

131 INT. JONES BATHROOM - DAY
131

BOB is standing in the bathroom, his face lathered with shaving cream, delivering another INSTRUCTIONAL VIDEO.

> BOB
> There are basically two schools of shaving, shaving up or shaving down. I do both. Down first and then up. Up is painful but women will love it. It's worth the pain. Trust me.

131A INT. JONES LIVING ROOM - DAY
131A

CUT TO A CHRISTMAS TREE and presents all over the living room floor. One present, a giant teddy bear hovers over BRIAN. There is a toy train, a toy car, a play house, and many other gifts. BRIAN however is interested in only one thing, the wrapping paper.

132 INT. JONES LIVING ROOM - DAY
132

BRAIN is sitting up, his back supported by a pillow and his mother's hand.

> BOB (V.O.)
> Okay let go.

GAIL lets go. BRIAN balances for about two seconds and then topples over.

Jump cut to BRIAN sitting once again.

> BOB (V.O.)
> Okay, this is for real, the real thing. Brian sitting.

(CONTINUED)

132 CONTINUED: 132

This time he lasts for about three seconds and then falls again.

Jump cut to a series of images until BRIAN manages to stay upright for almost six seconds but his parents' applause so startles him that he falls over one last time.

133 INT. JONES BEDROOM - DAY 133

BOB is in front of a chalk board diagramming a basketball play for another INSTRUCTIONAL VIDEO.

>   BOB
> A good way to force a three-point
> play is to use your off-guard to
> set up a screen, then release your
> point guard in for a lay-up.
> Chances are that he'll draw the
> foul.

134 INT. T.V. - JONES LIVING ROOM - DAY 134

CUT TO A VIDEO OF A COMMERCIAL showing a baby scooting across a carpet in his walker.

135   INT. JONES LIVING ROOM - DAY   135

BOB is sitting in front of the T.V. with BRIAN, who is also
in a walker. BOB is playing the commercial back in slow
motion and talking to BRIAN. BRIAN doesn't seem interested.

                        BOB
            No, no, watch. Just study what he
            did. It's easy. You can do it.

BRIAN just stands there. BOB seems dejected. Then
suddenly, to BOB'S amazement, BRIAN begins to move. BOB
jumps up triumphantly.

                        BOB
                     (continuing)
            YEAH!

136   INT. JONES BABY ROOM - NIGHT   136

BRIAN just starts to fall asleep in his father's arms. BOB
is singing to him.

                        BOB
            "Some enchanted evening\you will
            see a stranger\you will see a
            stranger\across a crowded room\and
            somehow you'll know\you'll know
            even then\that somewhere you'll see
            him\again and again."

Suddenly we hear another voice join in. It is GAIL. She
walks quietly into the room. BOB looks up sheepishly.
Their singing becomes a duet.

                     BOB AND GAIL
            "Some enchanted evening\when you
            see her call you\when you hear her
            call you\across a crowded room\then
            run to her side\and make her your
            own\or all through your life\you
            will live all alone."

THE BABY is sound asleep. The two of them look at each
other, grinning. They've come a long way to this moment and
they know it.

CUT TO BRIAN lying in his crib sleeping and smiling like an
angel. BOB and GAIL hover over him.

                        BOB
            What I want to know is, how come
            he's so happy? I don't get it. He
            doesn't have a Mercedes, a great
            job, or anything.

                                                    (CONTINUED)

136   CONTINUED:

>   GAIL
>   Maybe he's just happy being alive.
>
>   BOB
>   What does that make him...a mutant
>   or something?
>
>   GAIL
>   That makes him your son.
>
>   BOB
>   What is that supposed to mean?
>
>   GAIL
>   He's learning it from you.

BOB smiles. He likes that. He takes GAIL by the hand and they tiptoe toward the door.

>   BOB
>   I love you Gail.
>
>   GAIL
>   (smiling)
>   I know.

BOB reaches for the light and flips it off. We see them in silhouette for a moment as they step into the hall. And then suddenly, as if struck by lightning, BOB crumples to the floor. GAIL screams. THE BABY begins to cry.

137   INT. DOCTOR'S OFFICE - DAY

BOB and GAIL sit ashen faced in front of a doctor we have not seen before. He too looks very glum.

>   DR. ALTMAN
>   I'm afraid the cancer has spread to
>   the brain. This is not uncommon
>   with kidney cancer. It's very
>   opportunistic. The miracle is that
>   you have survived this long. I
>   don't know what has kept you alive,
>   but a man in your condition should
>   not be sitting across from me right
>   now. Traditionally a brain tumor
>   of this size progresses very
>   quickly. I hate to be the one to
>   tell you this, but there is really
>   very little time left.

(CONTINUED)

137 CONTINUED:

                    BOB
          What? A month? Two?

                    DR. ALTMAN
          I think we are talking weeks. And
          that's with luck.

GAIL gasps. BOB reaches out to her.

                    DR. ALTMAN
          We can hospitalize you if you wish,
          but in truth, hospice care can be
          equally effective, and you can stay
          in the comfort of your own home.
          I'll be happy to recommend a
          service for you. We'll also begin
          a series of cortisone treatments.
          It does cause swelling in the
          facial area but that helps minimize
          the pressure in the skull.

THE DOCTOR continues talking but we can no longer hear his
words. A terrible silence has invaded the room. We sense
it will never go away. Slowly BOB'S image begins to
dissolve in light. The light begins to pulsate.

138 INT. MR. HO'S OFFICE - DAY

There is a blinding flash of light and we cut to BOB in MR.
HO'S office. MR. HO'S hands are working gently over the
crown of BOB'S head.

                    BOB
          That light. I keep seeing that
          light. What is it? Why do I keep
          seeing it?

                    MR. HO
          That is the light of the Self. It
          is the source of life, the source
          of all healing.

                    BOB
          Does that mean it's working? Can
          it heal the tumor?

Quietly MR. HO shakes his head "no". Devastated, BOB looks
away.

                                              (CONTINUED)

138 CONTINUED:

>   MR. HO
>   It is growing too fast.
>
>   BOB
>   But, isn't there anything? What
>   can I do?

                                            (CONTINUED)

138 CONTINUED: 138

> MR. HO
> Put your house in order.
> (he strokes BOB'S head)
> Find peace.

139 INT. JONES HOUSE - DAY   139

CHAOS. THE BABY is screaming. DORIS, GAIL'S mother, is trying to keeping him quiet.

140 INT. JONES KITCHEN - DAY   140

GAIL is in the kitchen preparing baby food. The blender is whirring loudly. The doorbell rings.

> GAIL
> Someone get that!

141 INT. JONES DEN & LIVING ROOM - DAY   141

We see BOB sitting on the living room couch, staring into space. He looks strangely different, heavier, bloated. The doorbell rings again.

> GAIL
> (continuing)
> Does anybody hear me?

BOB hears her. With effort he stands up and begins walking to the door. We notice that he is holding onto chairs and tables for support.

The doorbell rings again. GAIL, furious, storms into the living room.

> GAIL
> Goddamn it, why doesn't anyone...?

She sees BOB standing at the door with a large, overbearing woman standing outside. GAIL walks to the door.

> THERESA
> No need to ask who the patient is. You're Bob, I assume. Hi. I'm Theresa. You can call me Mother Theresa if you want. Everybody does. And you're the wife? Are you Gail?

> GAIL
> Gail.

(CONTINUED)

141 CONTINUED:

> THERESA
> Hi. I'm your hospice nurse. Dr. Altman referred me. Theresa. Can I come in?

> BOB
> (his mouth open)
> Sure. Yes. Of course. Come on in.

They walk into the living room. GAIL motions her to the couch. It is obvious BOB is having trouble walking.

> THERESA
> We're gonna need a walker aren't we? I'll bring one over this afternoon. Dr. Altman filled me in on everything. I just want you to know that we're going to help you in every way we can.

DORIS appears with the BABY who is still crying. GAIL looks harried. THERESA looks up admiringly.

> DORIS
> He won't stop crying.

> THERESA
> Can I? Hi, my name's Theresa. The hospice worker.

> DORIS
> Hello. I'm Doris. The mother-in-law.

THERESA stands up and takes hold of BRIAN. In an instant he has stopped crying. Everyone looks at her amazed. She smiles and dances quietly for a moment with the BABY. We sense that her heart is as big as the house. She hands the BABY back to DORIS. He is totally docile.

> THERESA
> (continuing)
> Well, I'm not here to take care of babies. Not little ones anyway. There's a lot of other things to do. We have to work up a pain management program. Are you having a lot of discomfort?

> BOB
> (nodding yes)
> It's getting worse.

(CONTINUED)

141   CONTINUED: 2   141

> THERESA
> Well, we're gonna monitor you very
> closely. Our idea is to stay ahead
> of the pain, not run after it.
> We're gonna make you as comfortable
> as possible. You just wait and see.

142   INT. JONES DEN & KITCHEN - DAY   142

ANGLE ON A WALKER often used by the elderly. THERESA is trying to show BOB how to use it. He is having difficulty.

> THERESA
> Come on, that's a good boy. Just
> balance, lift the walker, and take
> a little step.

BOB starts to wobble. She catches him.

> BOB
> It's getting harder.

> THERESA
> That's okay. You're doing just
> fine. Patience. Take your time.

BOB looks very embarrassed by his inability to walk. GAIL glances at him from the other room. The look on her face is full of suffering and pain.

143   INT. JONES STAIRCASE - DAY   143

THERESA is helping BOB up the stairs. It is obvious after about four steps that he can't go any further. Terribly frustrated, he starts mumbling obscenities.

> THERESA
> No, no. None of that. We just lay
> you down in the den, that's all. No
> big deal.

She turns him around and helps him back down the stairs.

144   INT. JONES DEN - DAY   144

DELIVERY MEN have just finished installing a hospital bed in the den. DORIS is checking out the controls as GAIL signs the receipt.

(CONTINUED)

144 CONTINUED:

> DELIVERY MAN 1
> That should do it.

> DORIS
> Thanks.

> GAIL
> Thank you both.

> DELIVERY MAN 2
> A pleasure ma'am.

DORIS shows the men to the door. GAIL sits on the floor beside the bed and begins to cry. DORIS comes back and kneels down beside her.

> GAIL
> I want him...in my bed.

> DORIS
> You can stay with him downstairs.

> GAIL
> It's not the same.

> DORIS
> I know.

145 EXT. JONES BACK PORCH - DAY

We see a video of BOB sitting on the back porch overlooking the garden. GAIL is shooting. He is talking to the camera. His face is fuller now, swollen with excess fluids. It almost doesn't look like him.

> BOB
> So Barry said to me, "Do you want to meet a girl?" I was desperate to meet a girl. That night they introduced me to your mother. It's funny but at first nothing in me responded to this woman. I don't know why. Maybe I was intimidated by how beautiful she was. Besides she was too skinny, too tall. It just wasn't right. And she knew too much about public relations. Still, she listened better than anyone I'd ever met. I talked for hours.
> (MORE)

(CONTINUED)

145 CONTINUED:

> BOB (cont'd)
> She just let me go on and on. I don't know if I fell in love with her or myself. You've never seen such openness, such compassion. Even then I didn't think it was love. I liked her, that's all. But months went on and I kept liking her more. I felt good around her. I felt whole somehow. We just felt happy together. We still do. And then one day I woke up and realized, I love this woman. I don't know why. It just dawned on me, you know. So I guess what I've learned is that liking someone may be just as important as loving them. And if you like them long enough, what happens is-you learn what love is too.
> (pause)
> So...what do you think?

> GAIL
> (smiling)
> I think I'm gonna throw up.

> BOB
> Oh yeah? Well cancel what I just said. I pour my heart out and look what I get.

GAIL glances at her husband and gives him a long sweet kiss.

146 INT. JONES DEN - NIGHT

Rossini's "William Tell Overture" is playing loudly on the stereo, the part made famous by the Lone Ranger. BOB sits upright in his bed, his head flagging, trying not to fall asleep. GAIL is sitting beside him.

> GAIL
> It would help if you could sleep.

> BOB
> I don't want to sleep.

> GAIL
> Just try.

> BOB
> I want to die awake.

(CONTINUED)

146 CONTINUED:

>   GAIL
> We're not talking about dying.
> We're talking about sleeping. Just
> a nap. How're you going to keep
> your strength?

>   BOBBIE
> Strength? I can't even lift a
> toothbrush. Strength.

Suddenly DORIS appears dressed in her nightgown.

>   DORIS
> Look, I know you're trying to stay
> awake, but could you turn it down a
> tad.

>   GAIL
> In a little bit. He loves this
> part.

DORIS rolls her eyes and wanders back out of the room.

>   BOB
> The Lone Ranger rides again.

GAIL smiles.

147 INT. IVANOVICH 50'S HOUSE - LIVING ROOM - DAY

A BLACK AND WHITE TELEVISION IMAGE OF THE "LONE RANGER" plays as the T.V. show comes to an end. Suddenly two huge boots enter the frame and the camera tilts up to a shot of BILL, BOB'S father, as a young man. He looks down at the camera and smiles.

>   BILL
> So long pardner.

Little BOBBIE, wearing a cowboy hat, looks up at the heroic image of his father. He jumps up instantly and grabs hold of his leg.

>   BOBBIE
> Daddy, don't go. Stay home.

>   BILL
> Sorry. No can do.

(CONTINUED)

147   CONTINUED: 147

                              BOBBIE
                    Please Daddy, please. Stay

                              BILL
                    I wish I could. I really do. One
                    day you'll understand. Listen, you
                    be good to your mother. And if you
                    feel a kiss in the middle of the
                    night, it'll be me.

    BILL picks BOBBIE up, gives him a big hug, and carries him
    to the front door. There he sets him down in the doorway
    and heads out to his pickup truck. BOBBIE stands there for
    a long time watching as the truck pulls out of the driveway
    and disappears down the street.

148   INT. JONES DEN - NIGHT   148

    BOB is asleep sitting up. His face is covered with
    perspiration and we can tell that he is dreaming. Suddenly
    he calls out.

                              BOB
                    Daddy!

    His eyes shoot open. For a moment he is not sure where he
    is. GAIL, asleep on the sofa, stirs but does not wake up.
    There is a look of terrible longing and sadness on BOB'S
    face.

    With great effort BOB gets out of bed.

149   INT. JONES ENTRY HALL, STAIRS AND LIVING ROOM - NIGHT   149

    Slowly, he makes his way to the staircase, supporting
    himself with the furniture and leaning against the wall. At
    first he tries to walk up the stairs but he cannot make it.
    The camera holds on him tightly as he gets on his hands and
    knees and crawls.

150   INT. BRIAN'S ROOM - NIGHT   150

    BRIAN is asleep in his crib as BOB makes his way into the
    room and approaches his son. He stands beside him, holding
    onto the bars, gazing down on his sleeping child. Tears
    form in his eyes.

                              BOB
                    Oh God, Brian. What am I going to
                    do? I don't want to leave you.
                              (MORE)

                                                              (CONTINUED)

150   CONTINUED:

>   BOB (cont'd)
> I don't want to leave you alone.
> Please don't hate me for this.
> Dying wasn't my idea. Sometimes
> things happen. You can't always
> have life the way you want it. It
> just doesn't work that way.
>   (pause)
> My brother was right, you know. If
> I had lived I would have been just
> like my father. You would have
> spent your whole life being angry.
> You would never have known me.
>   (pause)
> Forgive me Brian. Please. Forgive
> me.

A look of deep sadness settles on BOB'S face. He turns around and heads back to the door. To his surprise and ours, GAIL is standing there. She comes over and hugs her husband.

>   BOB
> I need to call my parents.

She nods, smiles, and takes his hand.

151   INT. JONES LIVING ROOM - NIGHT

BOB is sitting on the living room couch. He appears especially weak. GAIL helps him hold the phone up to his ear. For the moment he is just listening.

>   BOB
>   (turning to GAIL)
> She's not taking it well. They
> want to know if I've had second
> opinions.
>   (back to the phone)
> Nom, let me talk... Dad, are you
> there...? Listen, just let me say
> something, okay. One thing.
>   (choking up)
> I never wanted to hurt you. I just
> wanted to tell you that. It wasn't
> you. It was me. The problem was
> me. I understand now. You did the
> best you could. I'm doing the best
> I can.
>   (he struggles to hold
>   back tears)
> I'm so sorry for everything. I
> just wanted you to know...

(CONTINUED)

151 CONTINUED: 151

BOB, unable to talk, hands the phone to GAIL.

                    BOB
                 (continuing)
            They're crying.

GAIL strokes BOB'S head as she chokes back her own emotion.

                    GAIL
            Mom, Dad. Listen to me. Just call
            back when you know your flight
            number.
                 (to BOB)
            I'm not sure they heard me.
                 (into the phone)
            Listen...we'll call you back. I'm
            sorry to upset you so much. We'll
            talk later this morning. We love
            you. Okay. Bye.

She hands up the phone. BOB and GAIL just look at one
another. There is a look of deep tenderness and fulfillment
in their eyes.

                    GAIL
            You did it.

                    BOB
            I know.

152 INT. JONES DEN - DAY   152

BOB is looking very weak. THERESA tries to get him to take
some food but he cannot get it down. GAIL looks at her,
distraught. The two of them walk into the hall. GAIL'S
face is white and drawn.

                    GAIL
            It's happening too fast.

                    THERESA
            It's a blessing. Believe me. I've
            been around.

153 INT. JONES DEN - NIGHT   153

BRIAN is sitting in his father's lap. BOB can barely
entertain him but seems happy just to stroke his hair.

153A INT. JONES LIVING ROOM - DAY   153A

GAIL is in the living room picking up toys. There is a
knock at the door. GAIL gets up curiously.

154   INT. JONES DEN - DAY   154

BOB is lying on his bed when GAIL walks in with a guest. It is MR. HO. BOB is surprised but pleased to see him. He tries to sit up but can barely move.

                    BOB
          Mr. Ho. I didn't know you made
          house calls.

MR. HO smiles.

                    BOB
                (continuing)
          It's good to see you. Only I'm
          afraid it's a little late.

                    MR. HO
          Not too late. You're still
          breathing, aren't you?

                    BOB
          If you can call it that.

MR. HO walks over to the bed and places his hands over BOB'S chest. He spends a moment checking things out.

                    BOB
          So, how am I doing?

                    MR. HO
          You're doing just fine.

                    BOB
          Fine? What do you mean, fine? I'm
          dying.

                    MR. HO
          We all die.

                    BOB
          Then how can you say I'm fine?

                    MR. HO
          Because I can feel your heart.
          It's open. It's healed.

                    BOB
          Healed?
                (he laughs)
          Great. Just when it's about to
          stop beating.

                    MR. HO
          That doesn't matter. Don't worry.
          Only the body dies.

                                                    (CONTINUED)

154 CONTINUED:

>   BOB
>   Is that supposed to be comforting?
>
>   MR. HO
>   It will be. You have to trust me.
>   Have faith.
>
>   BOB
>   (deeply)
>   I want to have faith. I really
>   want to.
>
>   MR. HO
>   Wanting is all it takes.
>   (pause)
>   You are a remarkable man, you know
>   that? You have made a great
>   journey. I never thought you would
>   do it.
>   (taking BOB'S hand)
>   I am honored to know you.

GAIL smiles and leans over to kiss her husband.

>   GAIL
>   He's my hero.
>
>   BOB
>   Still?
>
>   GAIL
>   A hundred times over.

Suddenly we hear a horn honking. GAIL looks up curiously.

155 EXT. JONES HOUSE - DAY

BILL and ROSE, PAUL and ANYA, are getting out of a rented car in the Jones driveway. GAIL, excited, runs out to greet them.

156 INT. JONES DEN - DAY

BOB looks up as the entire IVANOVICH family enter the den. There are tears in BOB'S eyes as he sees them.

>   GAIL
>   He's very weak.
>
>   ROSE
>   (running to him)
>   Oh Bobbie.

She leans down and gives him a huge hug. The others follow.

(CONTINUED)

156   CONTINUED:

                    GAIL
I'm so glad you made it.

                    PAUL
It's a minor miracle.

                    GAIL
I know.

THERESA brings BRIAN into the room. ROSE turns and sees him.

                    GAIL
                (continuing)
This is your grandson. Brian, this is Grandma Rose.

ROSE lets out a warm cry and runs to him.

                    ROSE
Oh, he's so beautiful. So beautiful.

She sits down, hugs BRIAN, and bounces him in her lap. BILL hovers over him proudly. PAUL goes over to GAIL.

                    PAUL
What can we do? Is there anything we can do?

                    BILL
We just want to make Bob happy. Just tell us how we can help.

                    GAIL
Sure. Of course. Just give me a little time. I'm sure there's something.

BOB angles himself up in bed and beams at his mother.

                    BOB
So Mom, you really did it. You flew?

                    PAUL
She was only conscious for part of it.

                    BOB
I'm so happy. So happy.

                    BILL
We all are.

                             (CONTINUED)

156   CONTINUED: 2

ANGLE ON MR. HO as he looks at the assembled family and smiles radiantly.

156A   EXT. JONES HOUSE - EARLY MORNING

The JONES house looks peaceful in the first light of the morning. Unexpectedly a truck pulls up in front of it.

157   INT. JONES DEN & LIVING ROOM - MORNING

Early morning light filters through the window. GAIL is sound asleep on the couch. BOB too is sleeping, sitting up.

Suddenly, outside the window, we see a bit of bright color flitting by. It is hard to tell what it is. Then gradually we are aware of sounds, the bustle of people talking, whispering.

All of a sudden, out of nowhere, we hear the blast of a french horn, followed instantly by the most joyful circus music ever played. GAIL jumps up from the couch. It is obvious that she has no idea where she is. BOB'S eyes open too. He seems very confused. Seconds later DORIS comes running into the room.

DORIS
Gail! Bob! Get up! Hurry up! This is incredible! This is amazing! Hurry.

They look at her in total confusion.

158   INT. JONES KITCHEN - MORNING

CUT TO A WHEEL CHAIR as GAIL whisks BOB through the house toward the kitchen.

BOB
What the hell is this? What's going on?

DORIS, BRIAN, and THERESA follow rapidly behind them. ROSE smiles and takes her husband's hand. PAUL and ANYA, still in their pajamas, hurry along too.

GAIL wheels BOB to the back door. THERESA opens it.

159　EXT. JONES BACKYARD - MORNING　159

AN UNEXPECTED FLASH OF BRILLIANT COLOR. To BOB's amazement about fifteen performers from a local circus troupe are performing in his backyard. It is the most magical of sights. Neighbors are running from all directions, still in their robes and pajamas. Music spills out over the yard and fills the neighborhood.

> BOB
> I don't believe... What is all this?

GAIL leans over to him and kisses his cheek.

> GAIL
> Your parents.
> (pause)
> Sometimes wishes come true.

BOB just looks up at his parents with the most unbelievable expression on his face. Never have we seen such joy. Tears run into the cracks of his huge smile. BILL and ROSE are beaming.

> BILL
> Better late than never.

BOB grabs his father's hand. PAUL starts to cry. Everyone leans over to embrace BOB, hugging and kissing him.

Families from all around are gathering on rooftops and peering over neighbor's fences. Children are sitting on shoulders and hugging their parents as they watch the extraordinary sight unfolding before them.

GAIL puts BRIAN in his father's lap. BOB holds him with infinite pleasure. He leans down to whisper in his ear.

> BOB
> Don't forget this. Don't ever forget it.

Performers in glorious costumes cavort before us, gymnasts, clowns, acrobats. Suddenly they come over to the family and carry them into the middle of the show. It is a scene of total unequivocal magic. Everyone is swept up and entranced by it.

160　INT. JONES LIVING ROOM - NIGHT　160

The family is sitting in the living room. It is filled with balloons. BILL is playing with BRIAN, tossing him up and down like a circus acrobat and whistling circus music. He revels in the attention. After a moment PAUL emerges from the den and turns to GAIL.

(CONTINUED)

160 CONTINUED: 160

> PAUL
> He wants the video camera.

> GAIL
> What? Now?

> PAUL
> That's what he said.

161 INT. JONES DEN - NIGHT 161

The video camera turns on. BOB is sitting up weakly in his bed. He is all alone. It takes him a moment to begin.

> BOB
> Brian. This is my last tape. I just have a few things left to say. As terrible as leaving you is, I want you to know that the time we've had together is the happiest I've ever known. Dying is a hard way to learn about life, but I'm truly grateful for what it's taught me. For what you've taught me... I'm just so thankful I've had a chance to meet you.
> (pause)
> Brian, I'm leaving these tapes for you. I'm sorry that's all I can leave behind. But with them I hope you will have a chance to know me, to know your father, as well as many children who've spent a lifetime with theirs.
> (pause)
> And I hope that one day you'll know that you've been loved more in six months than some children have been loved in their entire lives. I love you Brain.

He swallows hard, unable to go on.

> BOB
> (continuing)
> I'm done.

He reaches down and flicks the remote switch. The camera turns off.

162   INT. JONES DEN - MORNING   162

BOB is lying in bed. His father is shaving him. The scene is full of tenderness. They do not speak. We are aware that BOB is moving his lips. His father leans down.

                    BOB
          I love you, Dad.

BILL smiles and squeezes his son's hands.

                    BILL
          I love you too.

Slowly, BOB closes his eyes.

163   INT. JONES DEN - DAY   163

THERESA, GAIL, BILL, and ROSE are standing near BOB'S bed. He is breathing fitfully.

                    THERESA
          He's fading in and out. It won't be
          long.

                    GAIL
          Is there anything we can do?

                    THERESA
          Just stay close.

                    ROSE
          Can we help him?

                    THERESA
              (shaking her head)
          The body knows how to die.

164   INT. JONES DEN - AFTERNOON   164

GAIL is sitting with BOB, holding an ice cube to his lips. He tries to move his mouth but no sound comes out. GAIL leans close to him.

                    GAIL
          It's okay. You don't have to talk.
          I know what's in your heart. I
          know.
              (she kisses him gently)
          You are the love of my life.

The camera pans to BOB'S eyes. They are welling up with tears. GAIL wipes them with her sleeve. Suddenly he begins to gasp.

                                                      (CONTINUED)

164   CONTINUED:

It is a strange breath, different from anything we have heard before. GAIL gets frightened.

                GAIL
         Theresa! Theresa!

THERESA comes running in. Nearly everyone in the house is behind her. THERESA takes one look at BOB and knows exactly what's happening.

BOB'S eyes widen. He takes a short breath followed by a huge exhalation.

                GAIL
         Oh Bob!

She leans over and kisses him. Another tiny inhalation is followed by an exhalation that doesn't seem to end.

                THERESA
         God's speed.

The exhalation comes to a close. We wait for the new breath to arrive but it does not come. GAIL cries out.

165   EXT. ROLLER COASTER - DAY

The sound of GAIL'S cry merges with the sound of a roller coaster reaching the top of a huge track. BOB is sitting on it, holding on for dear life. Suddenly he looks beside and to his amazement there is the MAN he saw in the visions in Dr. Ho's office. The MAN smiles a smile of unbelievable radiance and warmth.

At that second the roller coaster rounds the top of the hill and begins its headlong plunge into oblivion. BOB clutches the safety bar. His face tightens.

With total exuberance, the MAN beside him throws his arms up into the air. BOB looks at him anxiously. The MAN smiles again.

                MAN
         Go ahead. You can do it. It's
         easy. Let go.

BOB eyes him nervously for a second and then grins in a moment of affirmation and trust.

CUT TO A CLOSE UP OF BOB'S HANDS as they release their grip on the bar. In an instant his arms are flying free, rushing high up into the air. There is a smile of total liberation on BOB'S face, a look of absolute freedom and joy.

(CONTINUED)

165 CONTINUED: 165

With a great shriek the roller coaster hits the bottom of the curve and shoots back up another hill. It is a massive surge that sends the sky rushing toward us. Life explodes into death. We are enveloped in light.

166 INT. JONES LIVING ROOM - NIGHT   166

A VIDEO IMAGE starts to form. After a moment BOB'S face appears. He is sitting in his winged-back chair reading from Dr. Suess' "Green Eggs and Ham".

      BOB
 "You do not like them. So you say.
 Try them! Try them! And you may.
 Try them and you may, I say. Sam!
 If you will let me be, I will try
 them. You will see."

The camera pulls back and we see BRIAN in his pajamas. He is sitting in front of the television listening to his father read. He smiles and points at the screen.

      BRIAN
 Da Da.

GAIL looks up at him sweetly and nods.

      GAIL
 Da Da.

BOB continues reading as the CREDITS ROLL.

      BOB
     (continuing)
 "Say! I like green eggs and ham!
 I do! I like them, Sam-I-am. And
 I would eat them in a boat. And I
 would eat them with a goat... And I
 will eat them in the rain. And in
 the dark. And on a train. And in
 a car. And in a tree. They are so
 good, so good, you see! So I will
 eat them an a box. And I will eat
 them with a fox. And I will eat
 them in a house. And I will eat
 them with a mouse. And I will eat
 them here and there. Say! I will
 eat them ANYWHERE! I do so like
 green eggs and ham! Thank you!
 Thank you! Sam-I-am!"

     THE END

Printed in the United States
2879